THE FABRIC OF MEMORY

EWA KURYLUK: CLOTH WORKS

1978–1987

Essays by

Jan Kott, Edmund White,

Elżbieta Grabska, and Ewa Kuryluk

Formations: Wilmette, Illinois

1987

This book is published as the first Formations art book supplement. Copyright © 1987 Formations. All rights reserved. No part of this book may be reproduced in any form without permission in writing from the publisher. Library of Congress Cataloguing in Publication Data
Kuryluk, Ewa, 1946-
  The Fabric of Memory 87-82024
  Catalogue of Works: p. 153
  Chronology: p. 155
  Exhibitions: p. 157
  Bibliography: p. 159
  1. Art. 2. Textile Art. 3. Culture.
ISBN 0-9618354-0-0

"Ewa Kuryluk's Book of the Body" originally appeared in Polish, *Zeszyty Literackie* vol. 4, no. 16, Fall 1986.
"The Membrane of Memory" originally appeared in Polish as the preface to *Ewa Kuryluk: Textile Works*, catalogue, BWA, Kielce, June 1981.
"Christ and Veronica" appeared as section 3 of "Mirrors and Menstruation," *Formations* vol. 1, no. 2, Fall 1984.
Designed by William Seabright.
Type set by Point West, Inc.
Printed by Braun-Brumfield, Inc.
Manufactured in the United States of America.

Contents

Ewa Kuryluk's Book of the Body, Jan Kott   9

Ewa Kuryluk: An Exile's Art, Edmund White   13

The Membrane of Memory, Elżbieta Grabska   21

Christ and Veronica, Ewa Kuryluk   26

The Fabric of Memory, Cloth Works: 1978–1987   33

Catalogue of Works   153

Chronology   155

Exhibitions   157

Bibliography   159

Ewa Kuryluk's Book of the Body

by Jan Kott

In Thomas Mann's *Magic Mountain*, Claudia Chauchat gave Hans Castorp a small silver pencil. Hans presented Madame Chauchat with an X ray of his diseased lungs. An X ray is light's penetration into the body. It over-exposes the body. As it reaches or permeates the skin, the ray of light outlines the body and brings out its shadows. Light's reach into the depth and its penetration of darkness are central themes of Ewa Kuryluk's paintings, poems, and writings about her art. "I sat in front of the mirror, covered it over with plastic and copied on it the outlines of my face," wrote Ewa Kuryluk in her *Journey to the Frontiers of Art* about the work she did in 1966; she then painted light gouaches, which since then have become gradually darker, and faces, which have since become longer.

In the conclusion to her article, Ewa wrote: "I draw on walls covered with thin lining fabric and I think of even greater fragility; that of glass walls, aluminum foil walls, of membranes, body tissue walls; of taking the drawing out of myself and pitching it up in space, so it would cast its shadow on the earth and on the sky."

Drawing as second skin, as the double of one's own face, one's own belly; drawing as the double of one's own pained body, as sisterly and brotherly doubles (as Ewa wrote, "the sister eye pupil surrounded by the brother white film of the eye") Ewa had taken out of herself; she had pinned it up on the walls, thrown it on wooden chairs and scattered it on the ground.

Villa dei Misteri was excavated in Pompeii. Its wall frescoes represent mystery rites, conducted most probably in honor of the goddess Cybele. The site, for centuries now covered by volcanic ashes and cooled lava, may have been used for initiations into ancient mysteries. *Villa dei Misteri* was the title of Ewa Kuryluk's installation in New York's Tribeca in the spring of 1984. Canvases were "draped," rather than pinned up or spread to their full size, on the walls of the gallery. They fell down from the walls much as a dress might fall down from the body. As in Ewa's poem about self-knowledge, from *Mistress Anima*:

Fine arts: a woman's dress
wrinkles and rears in no time
but the pattern settles
in the eye's mottle.

The face of one woman or of a man with her features recurs on most of Ewa's canvases. The faces look at us without seeing. Closed off in their own worlds and their own pain, sometimes they seem tortured beyond measure. The canvas supporting some of the figures is broken like a bone or an unhealed wound. On certain canvases the wound is sewn with a red thread which runs down into a chalice. Christian symbolism is evident in these icons of tortured bodies outlined or pressed on white cloth. They evoke the image of Christ's face on St. Veronica's cloth. Ewa wrote in another poem:

On Veronica's cloth
held by the eye
the red wiped off the face
glistens in the setting sun.

In medieval and Renaissance representations, Veronica's two hands lift up the image of Christ's head on the shroud as if he had been beheaded. There are two heads on those paintings: that of Veronica and that of Christ. Ewa Kuryluk imprints her own face on the white sheets of cloth. The cloth imprint of her face with eyes turned upward and lips curled in a spasm is held by her own two hands.

In *Villa dei Misteri*, she had also thrown her canvases on chairs. Her canvas bodies, some of them headless, were placed on twelve chairs, as if participating in some ancient and mysterious rite. Neither sculptures nor bas reliefs, the forms seem to be mere covers for bodies. Their skins look torn. Stubs of arms and legs protrude through their shapes. Women's forms open up like soft pregnant underbellies yielding to a scalpel.

Edmund White, who wrote about this exhibition, remembered Ewa Kuryluk as she packed all of her canvases into one small suitcase on the last day of the exhibition. Ewa Kuryluk's *Villa dei Misteri* fit compactly into one small case. Thin cotton cloth is the light medium the artist found for her art. One touch to these figures drawn on cloth, a dismantling from the chairs and walls is all that's needed to turn them back into sheets of fabric. They are fragile like the human body which, too, can roll up on impact like a rag doll.

For *Fall in Princeton*, one of the artist's subsequent exhibitions, she threw her canvases on the ground and scattered them on the shrubbery in the woods by the campus. Leafless branches poked and protruded through the cloth "bodies," obscuring and maiming the figures. Indian Summer colored leaves kept falling on the group. The cloths, covered with drawings of nude men and women, looked like bodies emerging from a mass grave. The cloth sheets were both bodies and shrouds at the same time.

Meetings of imagination can be astounding at times. Jerzy Grotowski had invited me to his barn in Irvine, California, for a nearly all-night show of his work with young actors. There were about six of us viewing the performance—far fewer than the number of actors. In a performance entitled "Main Action" and enacted in an empty barn, semi-dark with only the twinkling light of twelve candles lit on a low table, one of the frequently repeated scenes was a chase. The performers changed but there were always only two of them: the pursued and the pursuing, the hunted and the hunter—two men or a man and a woman. They were semi-nude, with heavy lines painted on their ribs, hips, and spines, with white cloths covering them as on Ewa Kuryluk's figures. Twice, when the pursuer caught up with his human prey, he covered it with a shroud. And twice the chased slowly lifted up his head and shoulders, freezing in a half-seated position like an Egyptian mummy in white bandages.

This past winter, Ewa Kuryluk arranged her shroud sheets on the snows at Princeton and in the Alps. She then photographed the shrouds. Photographs, even faded ones, are times frozen and preserved. They are memory. Memory's most sensitive media are photographic film and human epidermis. Ewa Kuryluk seems to have combined both in her most recent searches. *The Fabric of Memory* is an album of over one hundred photographs of fleshliness: of the epidermis/shroud, the epidermis/memory against the white of the snow. Even if this art, as Grotowski's *arché*, continues to use the imagery of religious rites, entombment in the soil replaces the Ascension to heaven. At the end of the Roman Catholic Apostles *Credo*, one prays: "I believe in the communion of Saints, the forgiveness of sins, the resurrection of the body, and life everlasting. Amen." Ewa Kuryluk's shrouds, covered by falling leaves or arranged on icy snows, seem to repeat a different prayer: "... communion of the body, resurrection of sins, and death everlasting. Amen."

—*translated by Daniela Międzyrzecka*

Ewa Kuryluk

An Exile's Art

by Edmund White

Ewa Kuryluk is Polish. Just before the declaration of martial law she organized the last international art exhibition to be held in Poland. She's a teacher, a critic, an aesthetician and a cultural historian who has written, among other things, a major study of Aubrey Beardsley. Her father was once Polish ambassador to Vienna and the publisher of Poland's greatest writer of fiction in this century, Bruno Schulz.

For most of her career in Poland she was an easel painter working in acrylics; I have before me a reproduction of a 1976 self-portrait, which reminds me of Alex Katz's portraits, although the planes of the face are more fully rendered.

Her international show, held in June 1981 in Galeria MDM in Warsaw, had the name "Garden of Knowledge." This garden, with its Edenic associations, Kuryluk explained in her catalogue introduction: "In all cultures the garden is the seat of the ancient goddesses of love and fertility, beauty and sensual pleasure, but also is the place of eternal return, of rest and annihilation where it comes to a metamorphosis and the mystery of existence is revealed." This vision of the garden of earthly delights in the Golden Age forms the utopia against which Kuryluk's later deformations must be viewed. It is the healing wholeness that contrasts with the terrible partiality of her later work.

While she was living briefly in London and painting in what she refers to as her rather "learned style," she underwent a crisis. One day in 1978 she "stopped seeing colors." Unable to continue painting, she returned to Poland and taught, first at the Academy of Film in Łódź and later at the Catholic University in Lublin. Although teaching art, she could not make it herself. As she recalls, "I wanted to draw, but not on paper. It took me almost a year to find this other medium of painting on cotton. I found I was getting interested in shop windows, in the draped cloths. I would stand in front of them for hours. Then I got myself a bit of cloth. Finally, the breakthrough came when I found this line of reddish pen, and the unbleached cotton that has the organic quality of skin."

Her first cloths were flat or taut and had scarcely any real folds. She drew in folds and nails. Even in these early cloths, however, an ambiguity is established between drawn hands that are slicing at the fabric with a drawn razor blade and real holes actually notched into the material.

By the late seventies, early eighties she was already moving toward the third dimension. Shrouds are draped and heaped up on themselves, cast on the floor. When stirred by the air they become ephemeral sculptures.

When Kuryluk was visiting Boston to organize her first North American show (she just had an installation at the International Bienale in Medellin, Colombia) martial law was declared in Poland. She stayed in the United States as a voluntary exile (with all the necessary weight of irony attached to the word "voluntary").

Responding to the need to pack up all her earthly belongings in one suitcase at a moment's notice, she now paints on pieces of fabric that can be draped over chairs or suspended from a nail or spread over a table (a still life of a just-finished meal) or folded softly within a framing box (a figure in a wood coffin). In her 1985 Princeton University installations, the cloths were tacked to trees and draped over brush.

When all of her works are packed away into a single valise, she becomes a sort of traveling salesman of the apocalyptic. The vision is scarifying and must be hidden away, exposed only on high holy days like some particularly foul relic, a bloody shroud of Turin or Veronica's veil impressed with the features not of the saved or the Savior, but of the damned.

Twelve chairs—ordinary chairs, anyone's chairs—are drawn into a circle as for the deliberation of Druids or the grief-sharing of the afflicted or bereaved, and over these chairs are draped lengths of cotton on which figures have been drawn in acrylic with felt-tip pens. Each time these pieces— lifted out of their hiding place like an old peasant's best embroidered linens—are exhibited, the arrangement is unique: new chairs, a new disposition of one chair to another, a one-time-only way of draping the cloth. A bare foot, exposed on a swelling bulge, suddenly bulks large; in a dark fold, a woman secretly begins a neat incision into her own lean stomach. In another piece, figures drawn in red are hung like skinned martyrs along the wall; a red thread dangles from a wound. Within a day an entire room can be filled with these harrowing figures. In seconds they can be whisked away, evacuated. Portable gods. Lares and Penates. Icons.

Or one thinks of Titian's painting, *The Flaying of Marsyas*, the gruesome account of the satyr who challenged Apollo to a music contest, lost and was skinned alive by the vengeful god. The curious mixture of lyrical details (the god's intense application to his job, the ecstatic expression of an instrumentalist striking up his violin) and brutal facts (the bleeding body, the bucket of blood, the thirsty dog lapping up the blood) remind me of the mood of Kuryluk's work, at once poetic and horrifying.

Stanisław Witkiewicz (1885-1939), the Polish philosopher, novelist, playwright and painter, foresaw a future state in which religion, the arts and philosophy—everything that celebrates unique individuals and the Mystery of Being—would be abolished by conformism and the strictly utilitarian demands of the state. As one of his characters says: "There's only one place for the metaphysical individual of our times: prison or the madhouse." Sometimes he fought directly against this drift toward the sterility and bureaucratization of existence. At other times he seemed to be collaborating with it, as when he started his *Portraits Enterprise* in 1925. According to the critic Piotr Piotrowski:

The creation in 1925 of the *Portraits Enterprise* made concrete earlier statements of Witkiewicz. He had affirmed that European culture was committed to extermination and that the formation of populist, collective masses, in which there would be no room for art (nor for famous people, metaphysical sentiments, etc.), would abolish the culture's fundamental values. In this "society" the place of the artist would be usurped by a producer no longer creating art works but fabricating the usual objects designed to be sold to satisfy the consumer needs of the new race. From this moment on, Witkacy (Witkiewicz's nom de pinceau) renounced the painting of imagination. He dedicated all his artistic activity to painting portraits to which he refused to accord the status of "art works." For the portrait, usually commissioned, functioned as merchandise in a manufacturer-buyer transaction; commissioned and purchased, it featured in a middle-class living room where it symbolized the social position of its owner. Moreover, it was a relatively conventional object. Nor is this visual archetype in any way weakened by the addition of a more "artistic" detail, which merely testifies to the greater refinement of taste in the particular client who commissioned it. The "Portraits Enterprise" is at once the manifesto and the fulfillment of Witkiewicz's own anti-utopia. It almost presents itself as a commercial production enterprise.

Fifty years later, Ewa Kuryluk may be responding in ways that owe nothing to Witkiewicz's solutions, but she is addressing problems that are, nonetheless, the ones he formulated. Like her great precursor, she is generating an ephemeral art that, paradoxically, affirms tradition. Like him she believes in the "Mystery of Being" (the phrase appears, as we have seen, in her *Garden of Knowledge* statement). Like him, she is witnessing (bearing witness to) the brutalization of humanistic values. And like him she has a conception of art that links it to the legendary past, to the realm of myth. Witkiewicz thought that even prehistoric human beings must have had a strong sense of the Mystery of Being (a fundamental intuition of the strangeness of existence) because even the primitive erotic experience is simultaneously an awareness of existential solitude and an attempt to overcome it. To him, art was made up of dangerous acts discovering and resurrecting this mystery. Just as Frazer in *The Golden Bough* has spoken of priest-kings who sacrificed themselves in order to preserve the vitality of the tribe, in the same way Witkiewicz revered artists (such as van Gogh) who killed themselves in order to fertilize with their blood our sterile age.

In a long, learned essay, "Mirrors and Menstruation," Ewa Kuryluk relates image-making and image-reflecting to classical, Biblical, and ethnographic texts; like Witkiewicz she has the same urge to place her work in a mythic context. She moves with bewildering ease from Polynesian cosmology to the Apocrypha, from Ovid to Lévi-Strauss. She quite specifically explores the associations clustered around Veronica's veil, which she concluded is both an erotic membrane and the membrane of memory. In addition, she writes: "...Jesus' pure and shiny likeness is fixed on Veronica's veil, a clean and passive mirror as delicate as an inner membrane. His 'true' portrait is a mask of death made from the blood that leaves his body in the hour of agony. This likeness, like a spiritual child, prolongs Christ's presence on earth and is a magic mirror that works miracles similar to those he performed during his lifetime."

Kuryluk's cloths are true symbols, not allegories, in that their significance is elusive but potent.

They are relics, but poor ones, not gold reliquaries, not wonder-working icons framed in jewels, not even stiffly embroidered chasubles. They have no intrinsic value; the materials are common, the scraps and scrawls of paupers. Nor are they fixed behind glass or over an altar. The church has been razed, the image slashed out of its frame, folded, hidden. During the Nazi years, when Emil Nolde was forbidden to work, he called his surreptitious water colors "unpainted paintings." We might say Kuryluk gives us "unconsecrated relics."

They are bedsheets, the lover's amorous tangle, fabric their writhing casts back, impregnated with their sweat, odor, the outline of their limbs. Lovers, Witkiewicz said, confront their isolation in struggling to overcome it; these sheets are signs of that separation and that ambition to merge.

Sheets also cover the sick, the operable, the dying, the dead. They are soaked in night sweats, fever sweats, death sweats. They conceal the emaciated or wounded body in a toga of modesty and expose its most shameful details in a clinging chiton of intimacy. Kuryluk's sheets not only cover the body; they also present it in a pitiless monstrance.

Here is the list: the sheets thrown over the corpse in the morgue; the sheets the lover draws over the exposed shoulder of his sleeping partner; the sheet the child wets and that must be stripped, carried off, changed; the sheet shredded into tourniquets, dressings, sanitary belts; the sheet that reminds the wife of her virginal past; the sheet that suggests to the virgin a future, of lust.

The French word *couche* means coat (of paint), layer (of society), diaper, confinement (during childbirth), bed (of leaves). These meanings stick to the experience of looking at the *Three Cloths* that were shown in a temporary installation at Princeton in October, 1984. The pieces draped over twigs or cast on the ground and photographed there had been created for an indoor setting, but the outdoors—the melting snow, the blowing grasses, the moving shadows of leaves, the changing light, the luffing winds—paradoxically animated these shrouds, materialized these ghosts. Caught there on twigs they looked like cast-off snake skins or tufts of wool torn off passing sheep by brambles or fossils of fallen deities or molds from which now-destroyed colossal monuments had once been cast.

Such an exhibition contrasts with a purely indoor installation such as the one designed for the Ściana Wschodnia Gallery in Warsaw. That piece, *Within These Four Walls* (1978), was a textile room consisting of forty yards of light, glossy artificial silk, a "portable fresco" showing the daily routines of a man and a woman within their room. Walls, as the artist has remarked, "have become more fragile than ever before."

Despite their mythic resonances, Kuryluk's works are pure products of the twentieth century.

Not because they use contemporary materials. They don't. They are a rejection of the steel, glass, and plastic favored by a Los Angeles sculptor, say, or the acrylic, abstract banalities of a New York painter whose huge canvases presuppose museum walls (the hushed sanctuary, the acres of empty space, the calm focus—art as the totemic emblem of a bourgeoisie steeped in "art history," alert to its microeconomics, eager to slow down the slide show of fashion into the only slightly more dignified procession of avant-garde styles).

Kuryluk's paintings, by contrast, testify in their very weave to their origins. Before she left Poland a critic, in a weird act of precognition, proclaimed her work to be "exile's art." At the time she was puzzled by the expression; soon she understood it in all its bitter fullness. An exile is poor; an exile lives out of suitcases; an exile has lost his language, friends, "contacts," context. An exiled artist does not fit into the aesthetic movements of the host country; she or he is not a participant in the "gallery scene." As Mary McCarthy has pointed out, whereas an expatriate changes countries for hedonistic reasons (better food, a higher quality of life, exotic impressions), the exile leaves home for political reasons and in exile remains focused on the motherland. The expatriate is a jet-setter; the exile is a Wandering Jew.

The exile cannot afford to practice an art that is parodic or conceptual or a recapitulation of earlier styles or a "bold rejection" of "prevailing trends." The exile's art must be self-evident, yard goods unfolded for the housewife's weary inspection, items that require only a glance to establish their history, their message, their skillful execution, their "soundness." Whereas the native artist may be able to indulge in a calculated ineptitude, a nicely judged barbarism, the exile must prove his craftsmanship at first glance.

Kuryluk's is also exile's art in that it exists in the tension between the compulsion to bear witness and the resigned recognition that no one wants to listen nor is there anything to say. Yet Kuryluk, the ignored Norn, goes on weaving her cloths. Her piece *Skin*, for instance, commemorates the night martial law was imposed when thousands of people were hauled out of bed and transferred to camps. The installation consists of ten cloths on which are drawn people's backs (shown life-size), some of them injured.

The sculpture of the Soviet masters, of all masters, is heroic in scale, cast in bronze, erected in public squares, didactic, sentimental, triumphant; the exile's art is portable, hidden, flashed at buyers like filthy postcards, dry-eyed, mute.

Kundera's novels show us individuals (their laughter, their loves) coping or failing to cope with a foreign tyranny; the books, although they take into account harsh political facts, are not "political novels." They are the opposite. They are about individuals; they are memories of people. In the same way, Kuryluk's cloths are created in opposition to politics. They are pictures of backs, hands, faces, parts of faces.

Or if this is political art, it is not of the

agit-prop sort but of the Kafka type, that is a fable threatening to come clear but always shying away from final revelation. Here politics proposes no program; it is a way of indicting crimes, not of handing down sentences.

Kuryluk's very medium, in making allusions to folk art and religious miracles, is politically charged, given the peculiar coincidence of nationalism and Catholicism in Poland, but never does her work signal a "return to the people," an arts-and-crafts revival; her sinuous style of rendering figures and her unblinking look at horror are all too modern. This is the true *arte povera*, a way of instantly turning any dwelling, no matter how humble, into a temple sumptuous with horror. Strong stuff, if we remember that "stuff" is also fabric.

In the middle of *A Thief's Journal*, Genet remarks that he writes in order to give his anonymous heroes, "the honors of the Name." Ewa Kuryluk is also engaged in this Edenic naming, although she's started out to do so only now, after the Fall.

The Membrane of Memory

by Elżbieta Grabska

One need not be an art historian to sense the proximity of Ewa Kuryluk's drawings and paintings on cotton to an old canon of European tradition. She evokes Veronica's cloth and, by doing so, points to her conception of art as a representation of our judgment about the world, as well as of our experience.

Ewa Kuryluk's technique reveals that both her materials—which assure the physical survival of her concept—and her method—which conforms to the structure of these materials—are subordinate to a meditation about human fate and her own destiny as she shares it with others. The figures she creates on fabric are self-portraits and portraits of people depicted in characteristic and intimate gestures. They are images which combine a meditative aspect with the nearly palpable sense of actual existence.

In her earlier works the painter resorted to specific story telling devices. Her energetic, raw, and synthetic compositions or portraits from the mid-seventies frequently included a quotation-like picture-within-a-picture, which added to each painting an ironic, witty, or bitter message. Stories about contemporary people were frequently "updated" by collages of pieces cut out of publicity brochures and magazines.

While close to the contemporaneous movements of pop art and hyper-realism, the artist's reflection on modern civilization was not, in effect, really derived from either of these particular narratives. Hers was a form closer to a parable. Each year, consistently, even if perhaps unbeknownst to herself, the artist has been moving closer to a moral poetics, aided along the way by her readings of, among others, Simone Weil and Malcolm Lowry.

In the dialogue between the artist's early paintings and the artistic traditions she tapped, the central theme turned out to be one of physical trace, an imprint, a "true image." This theme acquired a new form as the artist took up her experiment with drawing on fabrics. *Within These Four Walls* (1978), the installation executed on lining cloth in three colors (white, pink, and black) can be read as a morality play about the seasons of contemporary life. This was Kuryluk's first large-scale work on cloth. In it, the artist expressed the ambitions of a modern fresco with an ironic twist. She made obvious, on these thirty-meter-long cloth "walls" delineating an area of privacy, her need to articulate space by means of economic and nearly classical lines and to evoke it after the manner of the old masters. From today's perspective, Kuryluk's peculiar environments of this period, her "fresco lining room" and later her "tent-home" made out of white translucent silk, were harbingers of her later conception of a cloth as shroud, bed sheet and tablecloth. The experience of drawing the outline of a human figure against a neutral fabric background led her irrevocably toward issues surrounding the problem of a "true-image" ("vera icon"), a problem which modern art was compelled to confront in its review of the aesthetic and theological traditions originating with early Christian and Byzantine controversies over the icon. In the twentieth century several artists examined these epistemological categories and points of view which are related to notions of what once constituted "true image." These categories included revelation and resemblance, transcendence and reflection. But Ewa Kuryluk arrived at the cluster of problems surrounding the "true image" while searching for a new medium rather than through theoretical speculation. She did not follow the line of the twentieth century's radical iconoclasts such as Kazimierz Malevich or Ad Reinhardt, who both sought to reduce representation to its minimum or painterly abstraction. Rather, in fixing the contours of life, she found what Veronica's veil suggests: that the medium of cloth can capture momentarily, like the membrane of memory, traces of suffering and passion.

While beginning with what seemed most valuable within traditional poetics, Ewa Kuryluk was aware that the viewer would find her medium to be familiar. And yet her cloths, tablecloths, bedsheets, and shrouds seem strangely unfamiliar as the fabric used traditionally for canvases is called upon to carry the imprint of a figure or an object. Thus, the natural and familiar acquires a new expressive function while it moves back and forth between drawing, painting and sculpture. As for the viewer, the medium also makes for an extra-aesthetic experience, which might then affect an interpretation of the work or shape an intuitive comprehension of the artist's motivation.

Confronted with the representations on cotton or linen, one is tempted to apply the broadly used contemporary category of archetypal thinking, insofar as it covers universal yet subjectively felt intuitions. But this would not be entirely appropriate for an interpretation of Ewa Kuryluk's art or her materials. The cloth she uses is associated with physical closeness to the human body and at the same time it reminds us of more ancient cloths used on more elevated occasions of birth and death, evoking both the fresh sheet and the funeral shroud.

A long history of the cloth's utility reminds us that a fabric takes on traces of human existence while at the same time it remains separate from it. In the Christian tradition the traces became transformed into an image—and into a myth. Yet this particular symbolism of cloth, transmitted over centuries of moral readings, seems to have lost its original meaning once it came to be regarded as an artistic image or as an expression of the material nature of the fabric. In Ewa Kuryluk's operations on the soft, yielding cotton, and in the way she draws outlines of persons and objects, one can sense her intention to restore the original quality of the cloth and imprint, bringing out their utilitarian qualities. Still, in order to transform this frail and flowing fabric into a house, a table, a tent, an image of a loved one, or a parable, one needs first to master the material. In treating each new piece of cotton, the artist first devises methods which respond to her conception of the final image.

There are many approaches to the concept of memory. I would simply suggest associating the idea of memory with the act of making a drawing. I believe that artists who have an instinct for the illusionist image tend to, if not always consciously, refer back to their personal memory in a search for balance between the pursuit of the unique and a longing to transcend the unique by relying on collective memory. These two impulses have different intensities, either mimicking the fast, changing pulse of life or, as in the case of Kuryluk's latest works, taking one into a quiet and contemplative state. Sometimes the quiet is so great that it disturbs.

Kuryluk's drawings of people and objects

occasionally seem to be shadows or projections. They appear indifferent to their own physicality but are, nonetheless, sensuous. If the figure's fleshiness seems subtly devalued by the artist, it appears amplified by the expressiveness of gestures. Ewa Kuryluk speaks of herself most clearly in that characteristic gesture of upraised hands which hold a cloth on which is drawn an equally sensuous and ascetic self-portrait.

Suspension between the particular practice of real life and a general meditation on human fate characterizes all of the artist's compositions and portraits. This ambiguity is also present in her representations of objects, ordinary things, such as those we would use every day on a tablecloth. But when a real tablecloth becomes a background for still lifes they begin to mystify us by turning into paraphrases of objects. By drawing the outlines of the table setting on the tablecloth, the artist mixes the printed tablecloth pattern with the contours of depicted objects and refers ironically to the old artistic heritage of still lifes rendered in rich, sensuous painting which instructs the viewer in matters of illusion and "taste," in ways of visual "palpability." Conveying fleshly beauty, the painted objects appear to be within the hand's reach, within the space suggested by a tabletop or sideboard when viewed at eye's height. Such still lifes rely on the strength of illusionistic painting—an art which was once considered to be superior to all others—and the use of perspective.

Alluding to this second aspect, Ewa Kuryluk mockingly leads our eyes toward a real tablecloth laid down on a real table, and toward the ascetic outlines of a still life drawn directly on the cloth. She does not relinquish the magic of traditional make-believe but she does give it a new content. Her peculiar shortcut, and her distinct outlines, create the visual illusion of a table setting, of disembodied nourishment. The artist plays down the particular genre's tradition and plays up the content of our instincts: our desire, our hunger, perhaps even our aesthetic habits. As she unteaches us the habit of satiation, she also instructs us about the tablecloth's significance as companion to our brief, unceremonious meals, such as those one has when alone or while traveling. She sensitizes us to both the beauty of the drawing itself and the very concept of perspective.

Are the cloths, shrouds, sheets, and veils a philosophical adventure offered to the viewer? A possibility for reflection whose point of departure is both familiar and palpable? For it is cloth which, after centuries of closeness with the human body, acquires, thanks to the artist's imagination, new existential and ritual dimensions and becomes a symbol and medium for tracing the passing of the artist's and of our own time.

—translated by Daniela Międzyrzecka

Christ and Veronica

by Ewa Kuryluk

A Roman marble relief (ca. 400 A.D.), today in the Vatican collection, shows two seemingly independent scenes. On the left, Saint Peter is causing water to flow from the wall of his prison; on the right, Christ is healing the woman with the issue of blood. The second representation depicts one of Christ's miracles described in the New Testament (Mt. 9:20-22; Mk. 5:25-34; Lk. 8:41-48). It happened in Capharnaum where Jesus was asked by the chief of the synogogue to heal his dying child, a daughter of twelve years. On the way to her house, Jesus was approached by a woman who for twelve years had been suffering from the issue of blood, i.e., from constant menstruation. She touched his garments and immediately the flux of blood stopped. Though Jesus did not see the woman, he felt her touch and asked: "Who touched me?" Peter replied it was simply the crowd that was pressing him. However, Jesus insisted that somebody in particular had touched him because he felt a force going out of himself. Thereupon the woman threw herself at his feet and declared in front of everybody that she had been instantly healed.

The double composition of the relief expresses a coincidence of oppositions: Christ causes blood to stop; his disciple, Peter, present at the miraculous healing of the menstruating woman, makes water flow. There is also an opposition in the character of the two fluids: Menstrual blood is impure and the sign of a disease; the water is a symbol of life and purity. Christ brings the woman back to life by stopping the unclean flux. Peter animates the dead dry wall of the prison by making it flow with water—the pure life-giving element. Both scenes refer to spiritual strength personified in the figures of the two saints who are capable of casting away the impure and bringing the sick and dead to life. The miracles performed by them are victories of the superior male over the inferior female, embodied in the menstruating woman and in the inanimate matter. Goodness triumphs over evil in the Manichean sense that equates spirituality with perfection and materiality with wickedness.

When performing the miracle, the saints come in contact with the impure. To stop the flux of blood, Christ has to be touched; only at that moment a spiritual force emanates from his body and enters the woman. She approaches him from the back and they touch each other without looking into each other's eyes. There is a highly emotional and erotic momentum in this "touching" that recalls the moment of Christ's conception—the penetration of the Holy Spirit into the womb of the Virgin Mary. This association is made even more evocative by the fact that the woman suffered from her prolonged menstruation for twelve years: the age of the dying girl whom Christ was supposed to cure, which is also the age when menstruation usually begins.

While the Evangelists do not mention the name of the woman, later sources give it as Berenice or Veronica. In his *History of the Church* (325 A.D.), Bishop Eusebius of Cesarea describes a bronze statue of Christ healing Berenice which was put up by this very woman in front of her house in Cesarea Philippi, the home town of both Eusebius and Berenice. This statute is also mentioned in the apocryphal *Acts of Pilate* and in the *Apocritus* of Macarius of Magnesia.

It seems that the very name "Veronica" ("vera icon" = "true image") promoted the crystallization of a legend we are familiar with: that of Veronica who, on Christ's way to Golgotha, swept his face with her veil or cloth and thus came into possession of a miraculous impression. This story, however, which is contained for example in Roger D'Argenteuil's *Bible en françois* (a thirteenth-century didactic work) is the product of the late Middle Ages. Only gradually did Veronica, the woman with the issue of blood, become identified with the recipient of the miraculous image.

In the *Death of Pilate*, a short Latin text from the seventh or eighth century, Veronica is described as both an art lover and a woman fond of Christ. Realizing that he is about to leave her, she decided to have his portrait painted. But on her way to the painter, she met Jesus who took the canvas out of her hands and imprinted his face on it. In the *Healing of Tiberius* and its Anglo-Saxon variant, the *Avenging of the Saviour*, Veronica becomes synonymous with the "Hemorrhissa" of the Gospels. Thus the woman cured by Christ from her permanent flux of blood becomes one with the possessor of Christ's "true image" made, according to the legend, from his sweat and blood.

There is a strong sexual component to the miracle. In real life menstruation stops because of interference of a male and this announces the beginning of pregnancy. This may well by why the popular imagination transformed the cured woman of the Gospels into one on intimate terms with Christ. Because she was fond of him, she wanted to have his portrait, and it followed that he gave her the "true image." The legend developed into a curious reciprocity: The man who stopped the female flux of blood had before his death his own flux of blood; partly stopped by Veronica's intervention, the blood created a miraculous image, Christ's only true portrait. Thus, an intimate transference of blood took place. And with the blood, the material, earthly and female part left the incarnated god. The menstrual blood of Mary, "stopped" by the interference of the Holy Ghost, impregnated the cloth of Veronica whom Christ cured from menstruation as if by intercourse. Jesus left no offspring but he deposited on a female veil—an obvious symbol of the hymen—a true likeness of himself: the image of his earthly self, his female anima.

The face imprinted on Veronica's cloth is a reversed image—a mirror image—a "cloud of blood" which penetrated "deeply all over" the surface of the mirror. The face of Christ, an active mirror so luminous that it could not be rendered by an artist, was fixed on a piece of white cloth as if captured by means of reflection. Veronica's veil acted as a pure passive mirror which, being stained by the divine emanation, caught God's human reflection (his earthly soul) and became, consequently, the "vera icon," the true picture of God's incarnation, his presence on earth and his intimate relationship with humanity, in general, and with femininity, in particular. The woman whom Christ had healed from her flux of blood became so fond of him that she wanted to preserve his likeness. In this way the story reminds us of the Greek Cora, who outlined the shadow of her lover before he left for war and, subsequently, came to be regarded as the first female artist. The cloth of Veronica, itself called "Veronica," is a mirror image. The fact that a mirror multiplies images may be one more reason for establishing a connection between reflection, sexuality, and procreation.

The representations of Veronica with her cloth, frequent in medieval art, convey a delicate eroticism. The face of Christ hangs over her womb like a portrait of a beloved man—a son, a lover or a husband. Because of its photographic likeness, the motif has a modern counterpart: It reminds one of contemporary women displaying the photographs of their men in front of prisons or government offices to protest the disappearance of those who, deeply imprinted in their memory, will never die for them. These true images are outer shells of affection and intimacy. Like a woman demonstrating the crimes of a military junta, Veronica shows to the world the likeness of her beloved—an ultimate proof of existence.

Ewa Kuryluk with *Seven Black Chairs in the Snow*,
installation at Princeton University,
January 1985

THE FABRIC OF MEMORY

Ewa Kuryluk: Cloth Works

1978–1987

My work is about images which memory projects onto fabric and which the fabric's folding transforms. It is also about photography: about the ephemeral as it is shot by the camera and imprinted on paper.

Ewa Kuryluk

Indoor Installations

1978–1987

Cloths and Curtains

1978–1979

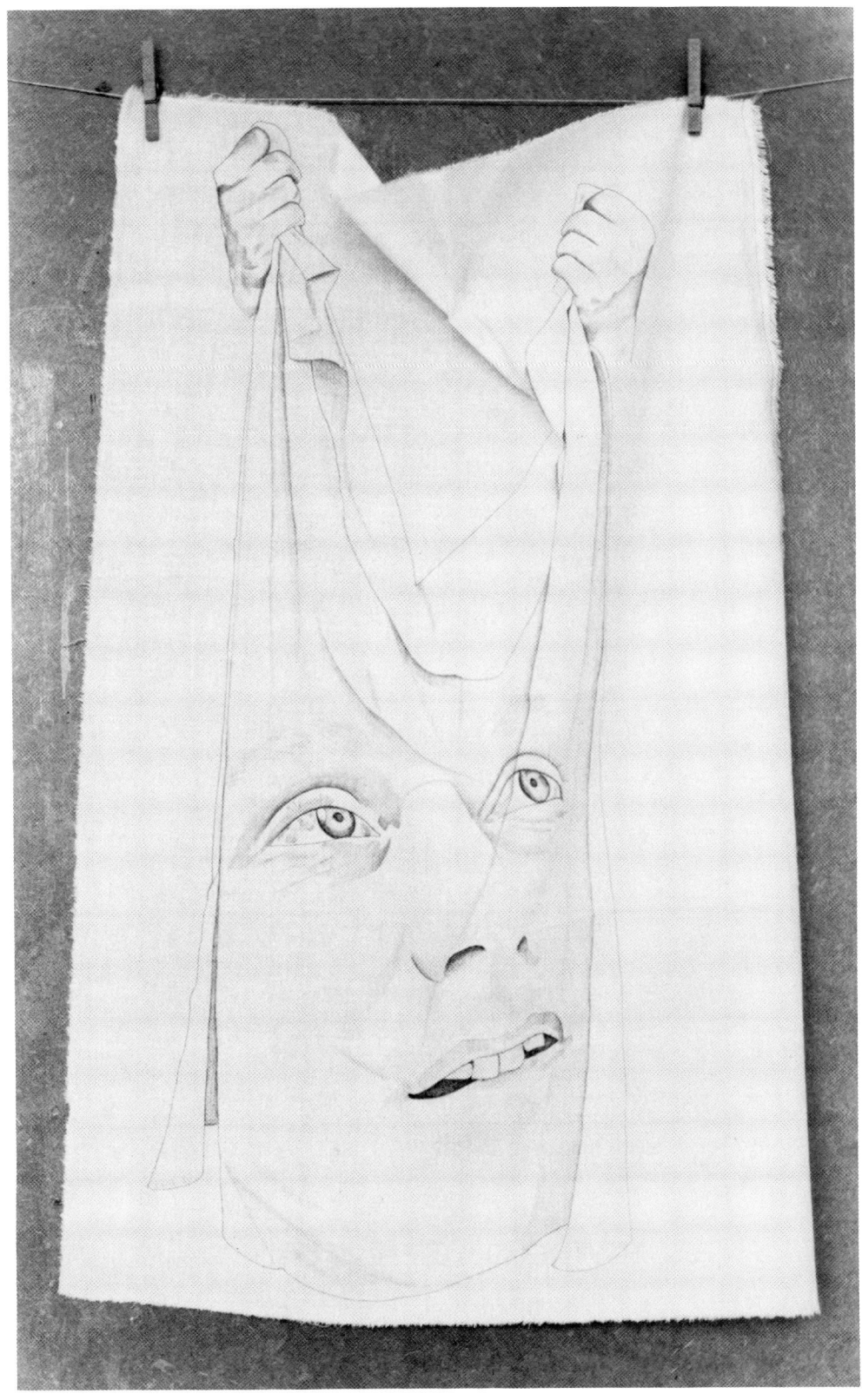

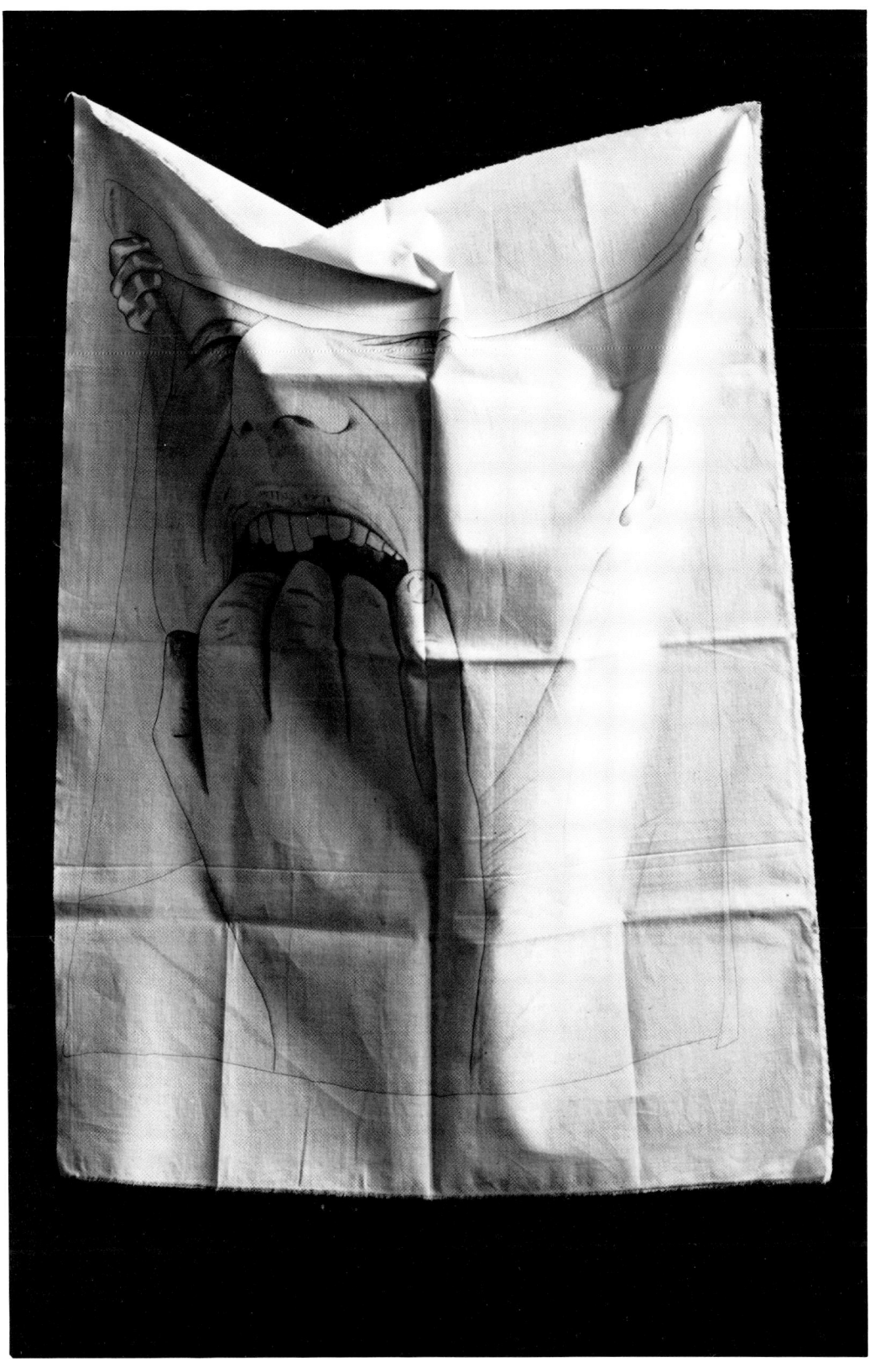

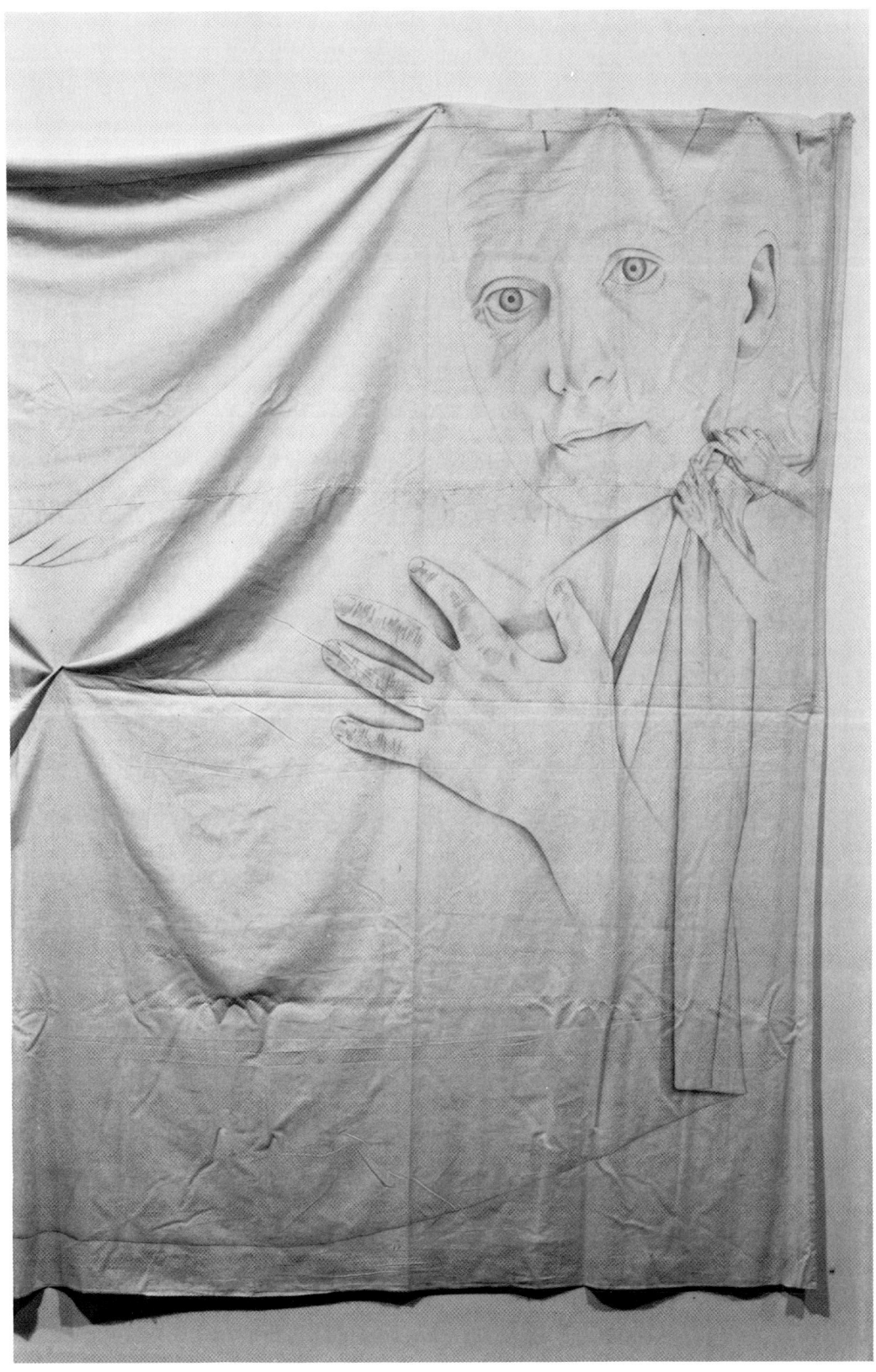

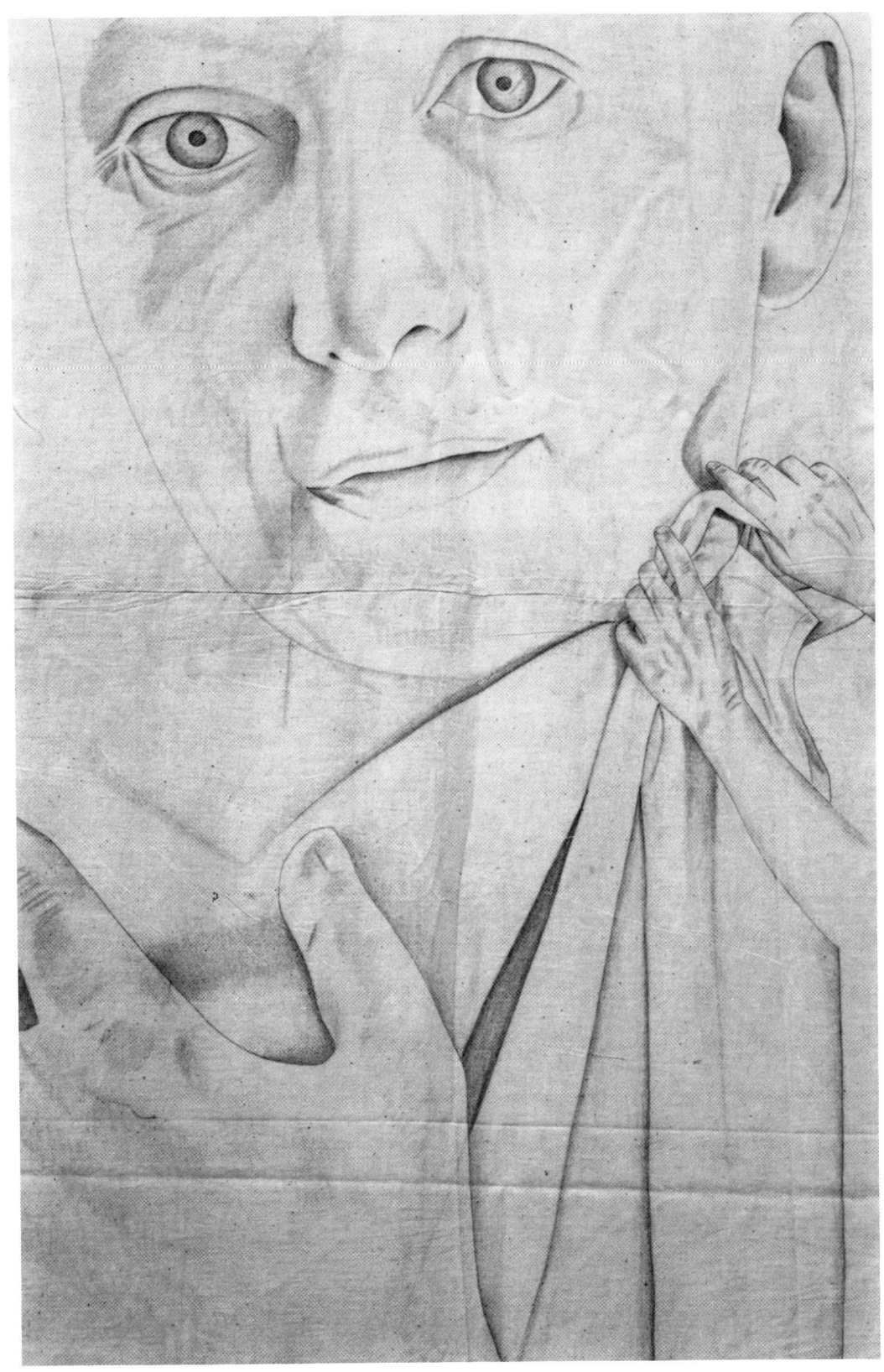

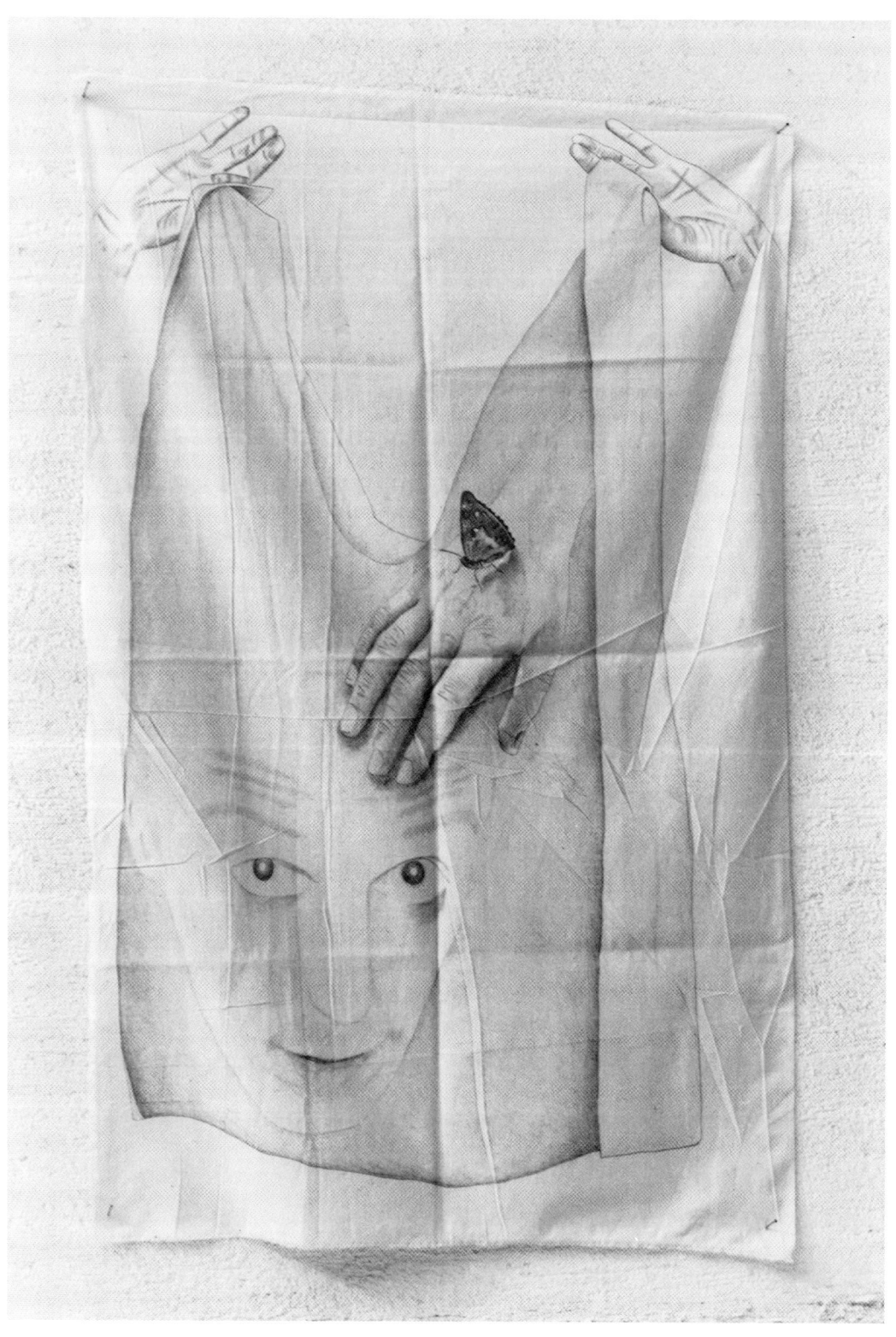

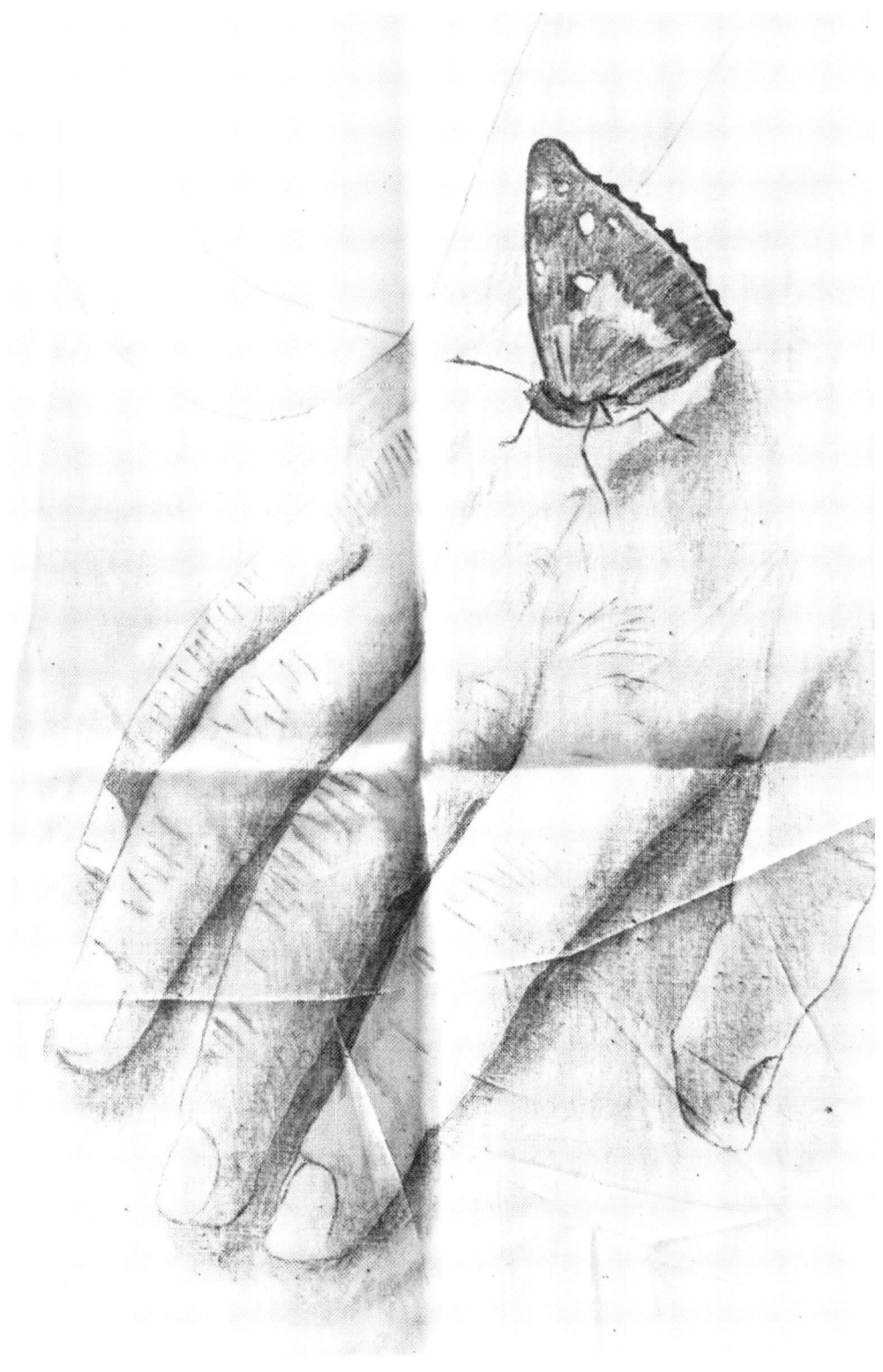

Still Lives

1978–1983

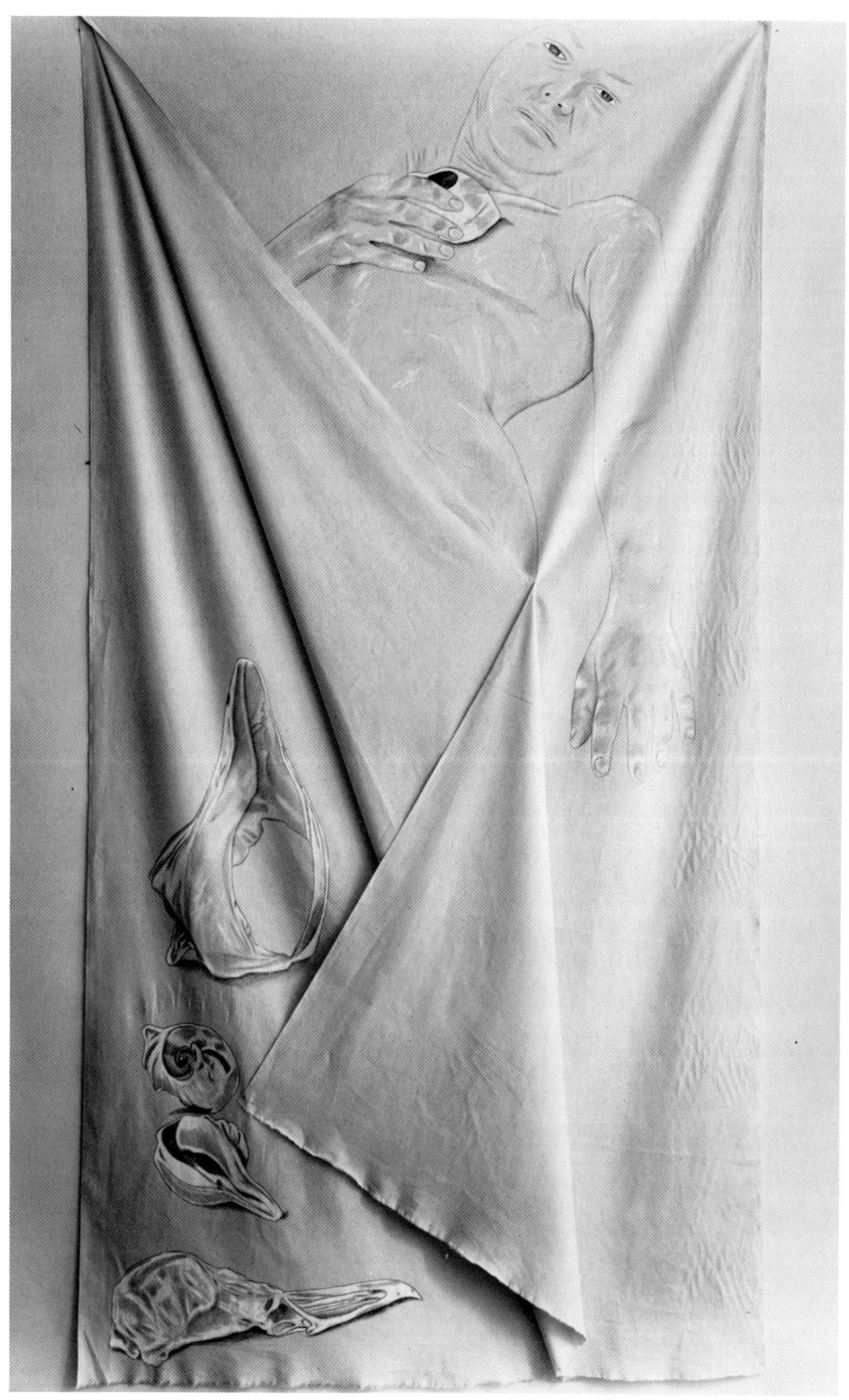

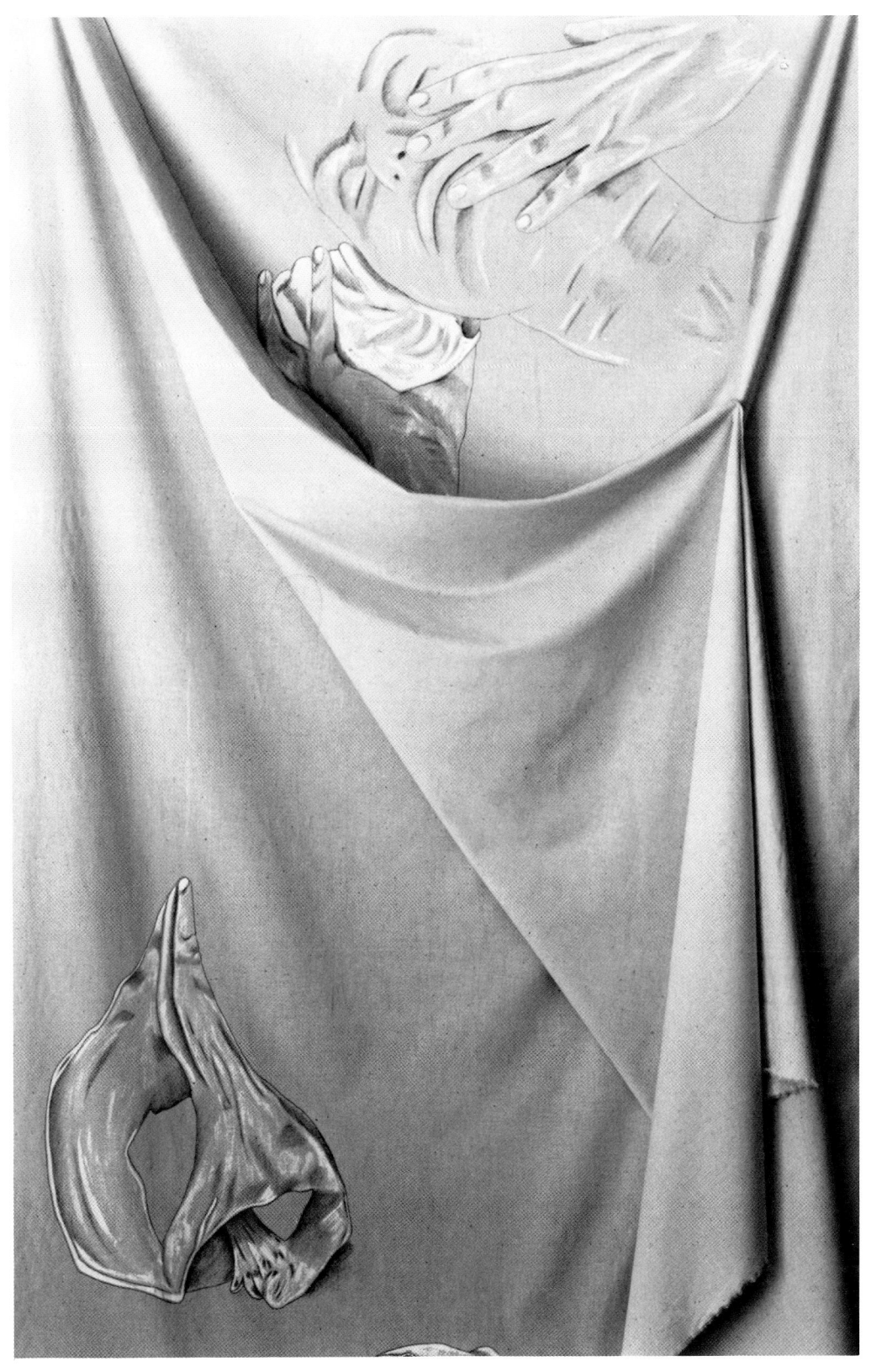

Theater of Love

1981–1987

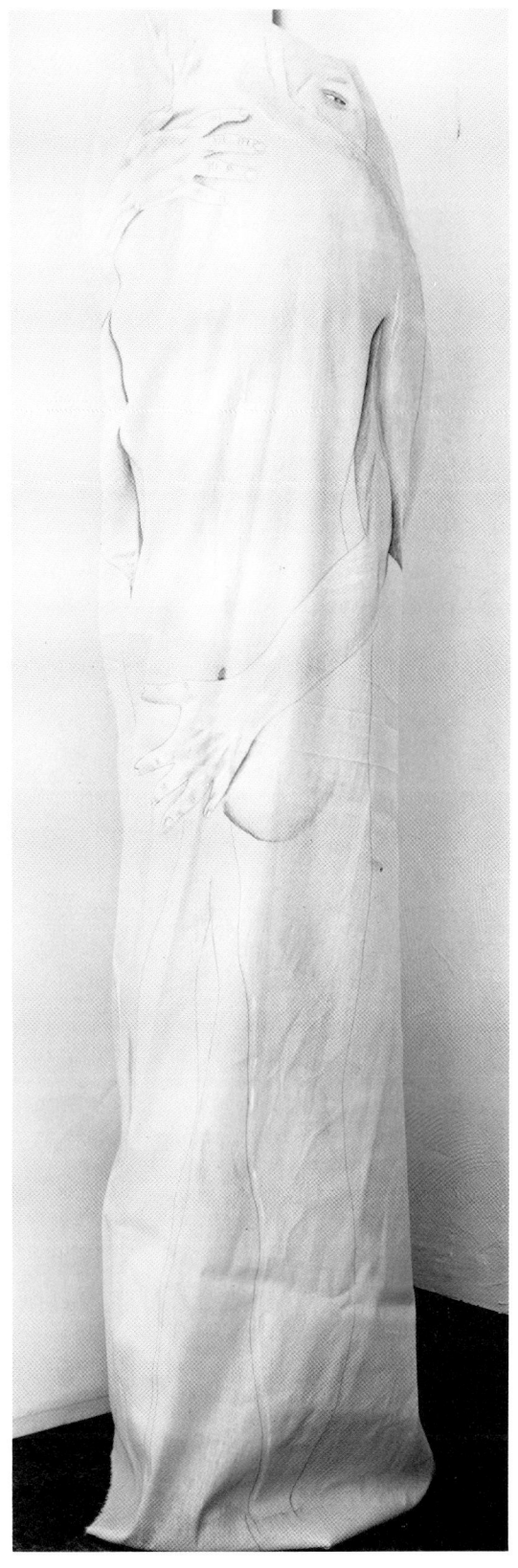

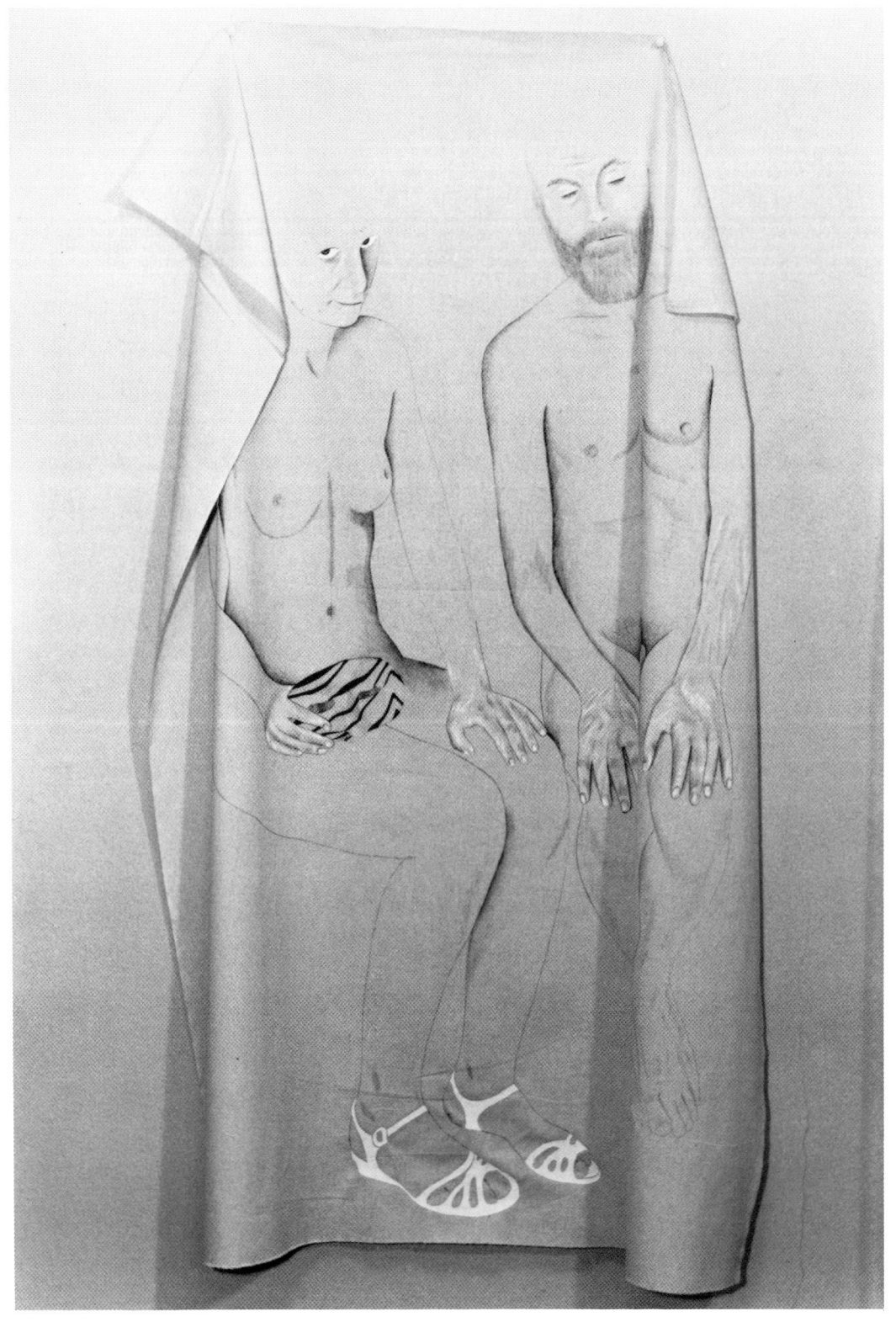

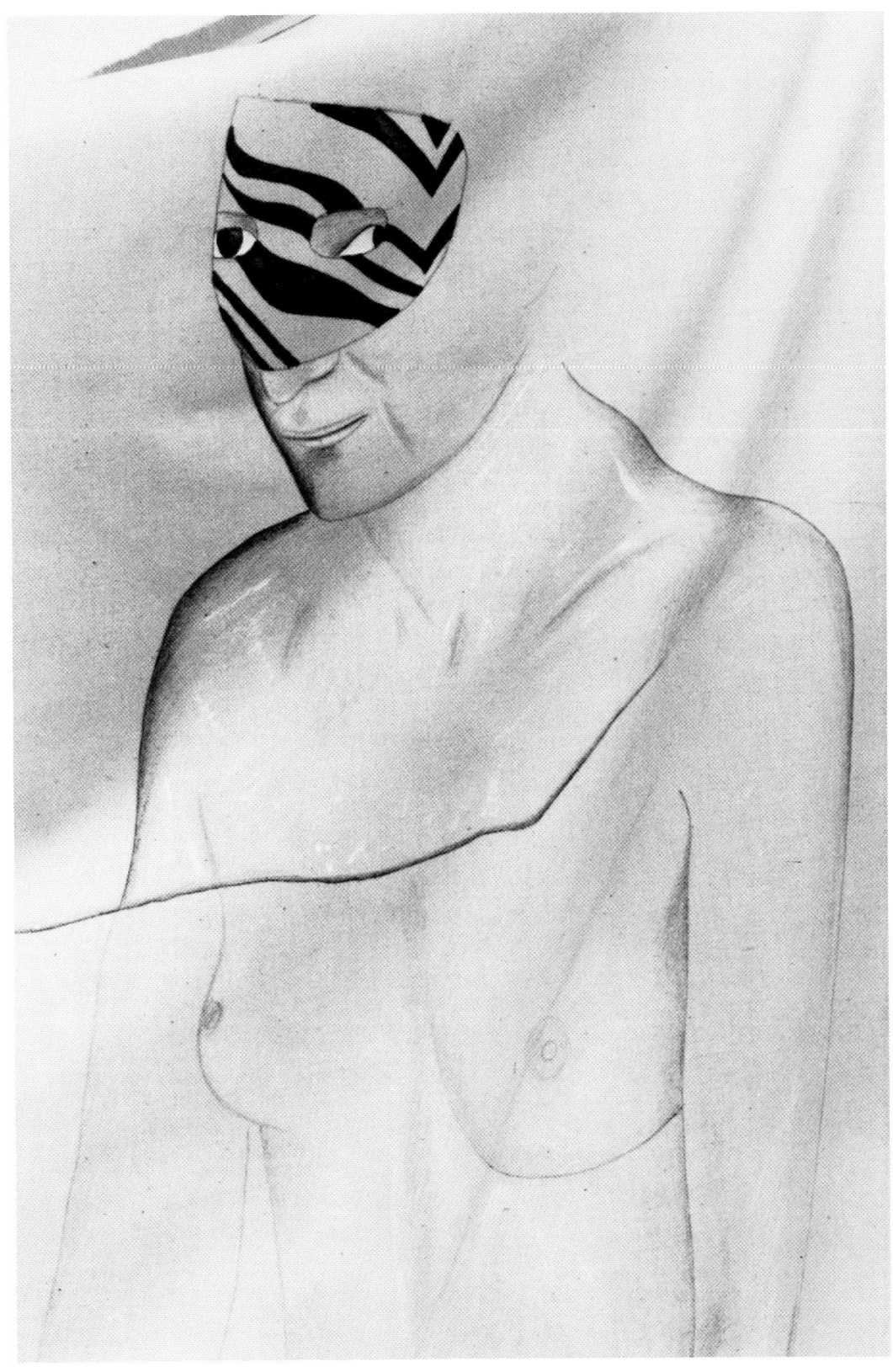

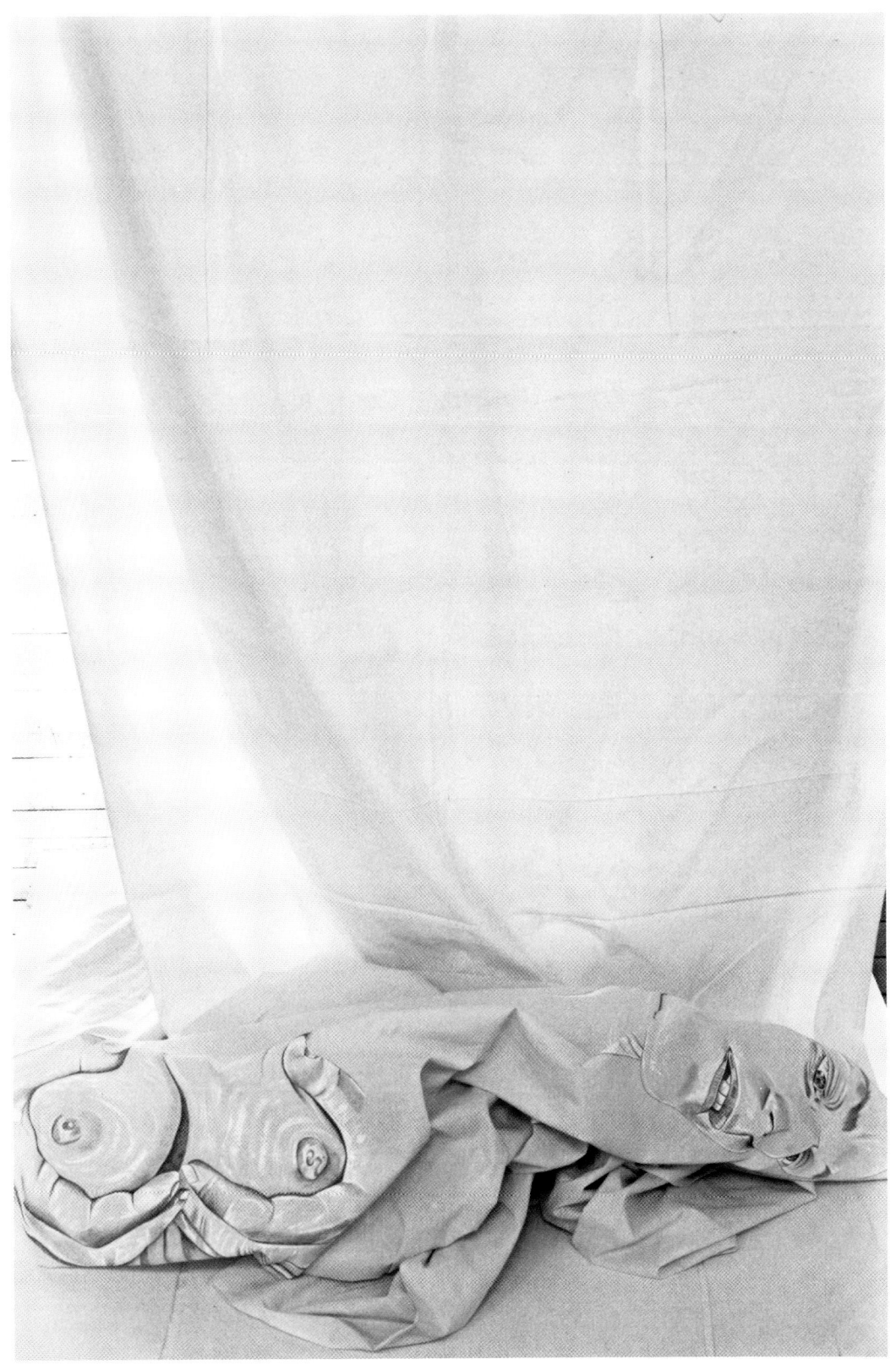

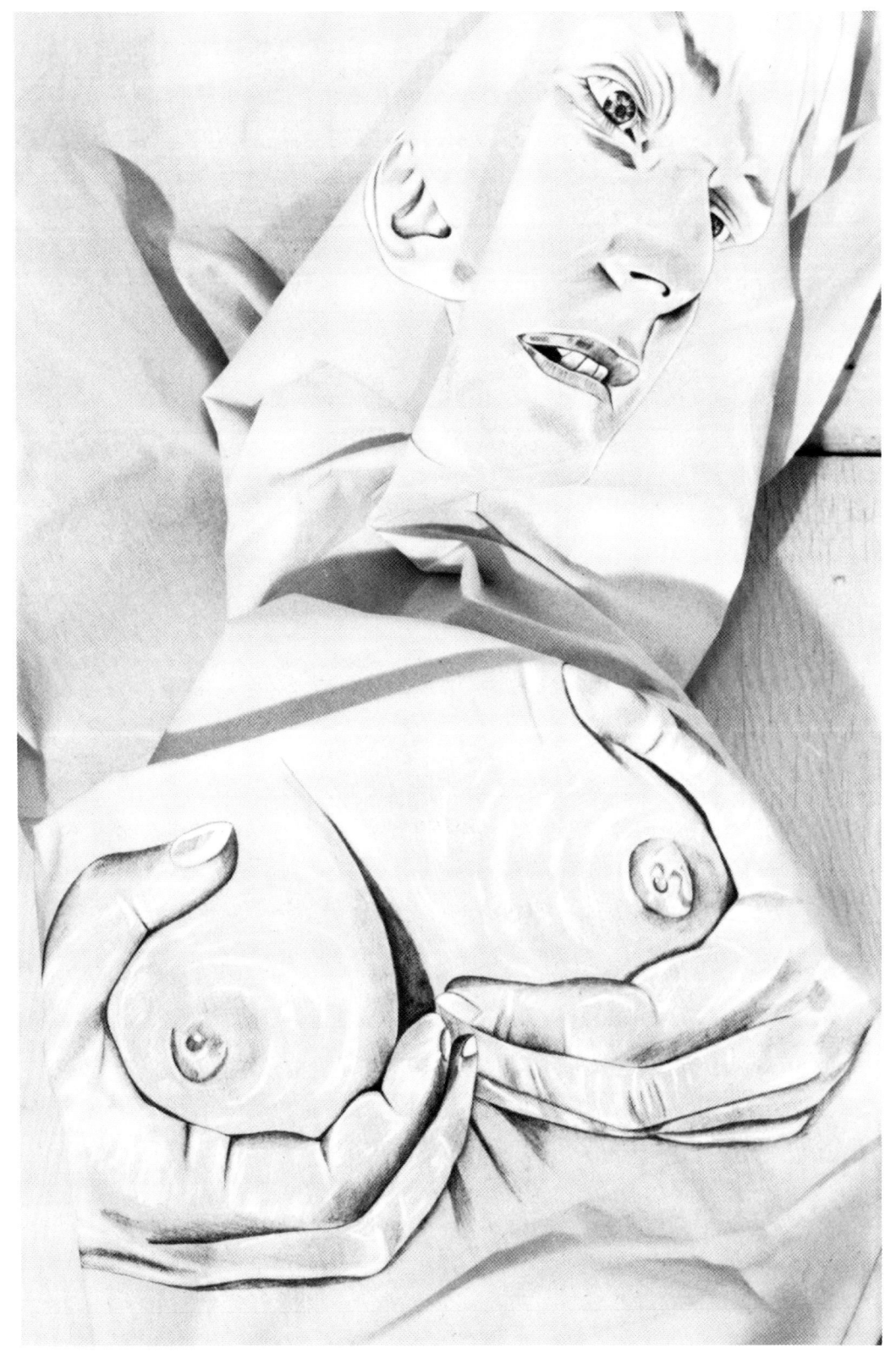

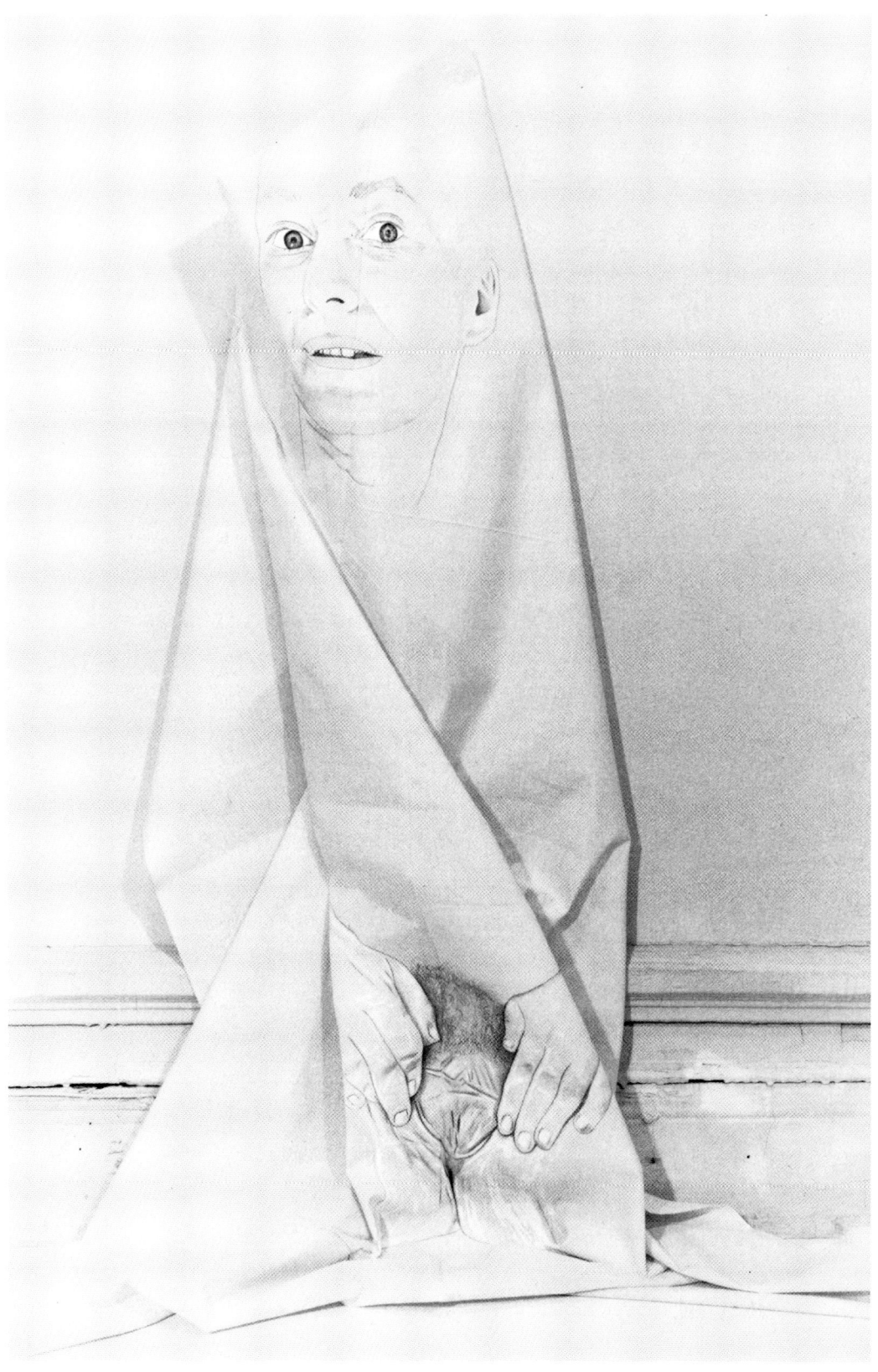

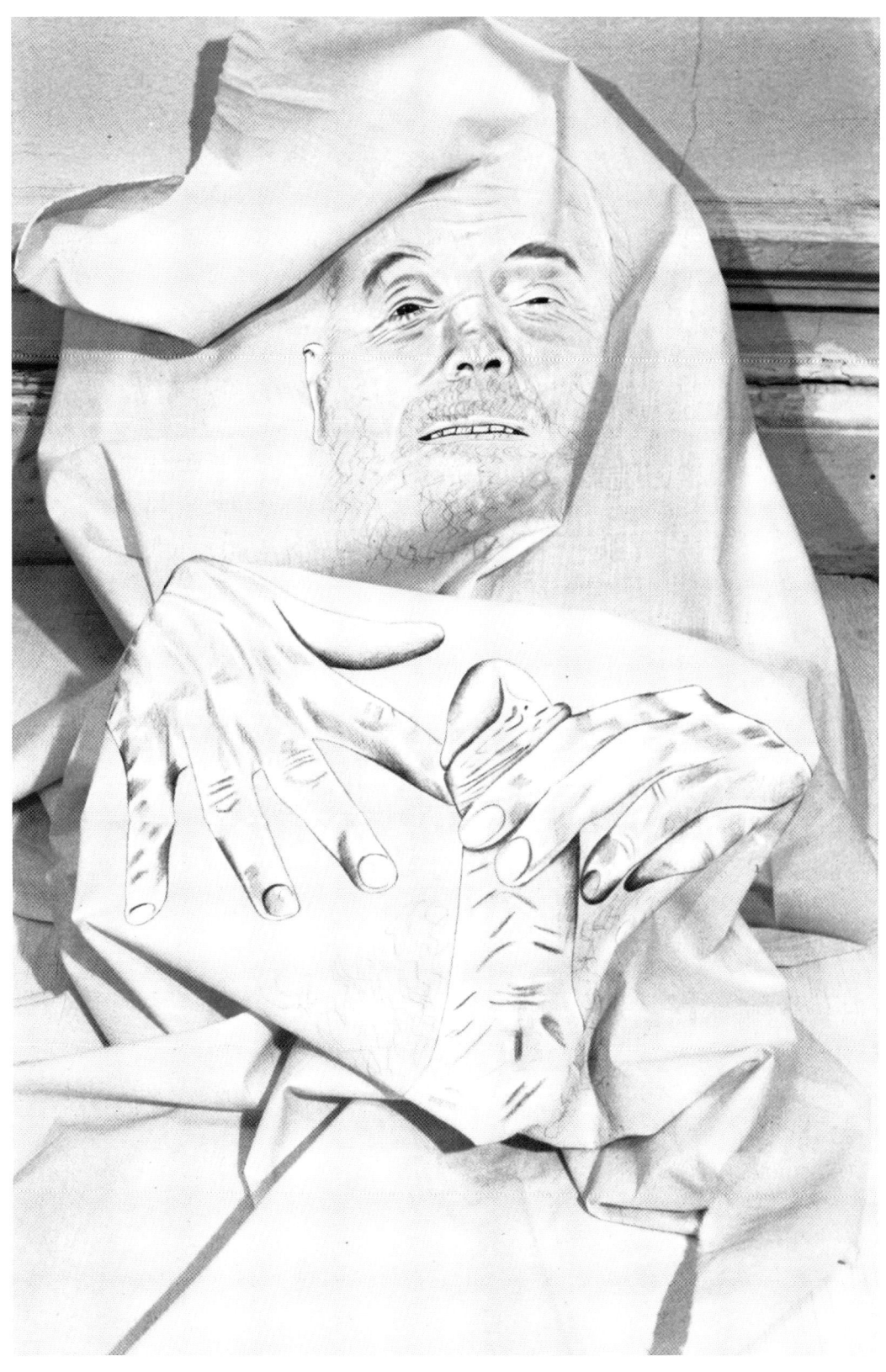

Figures

1979–1986

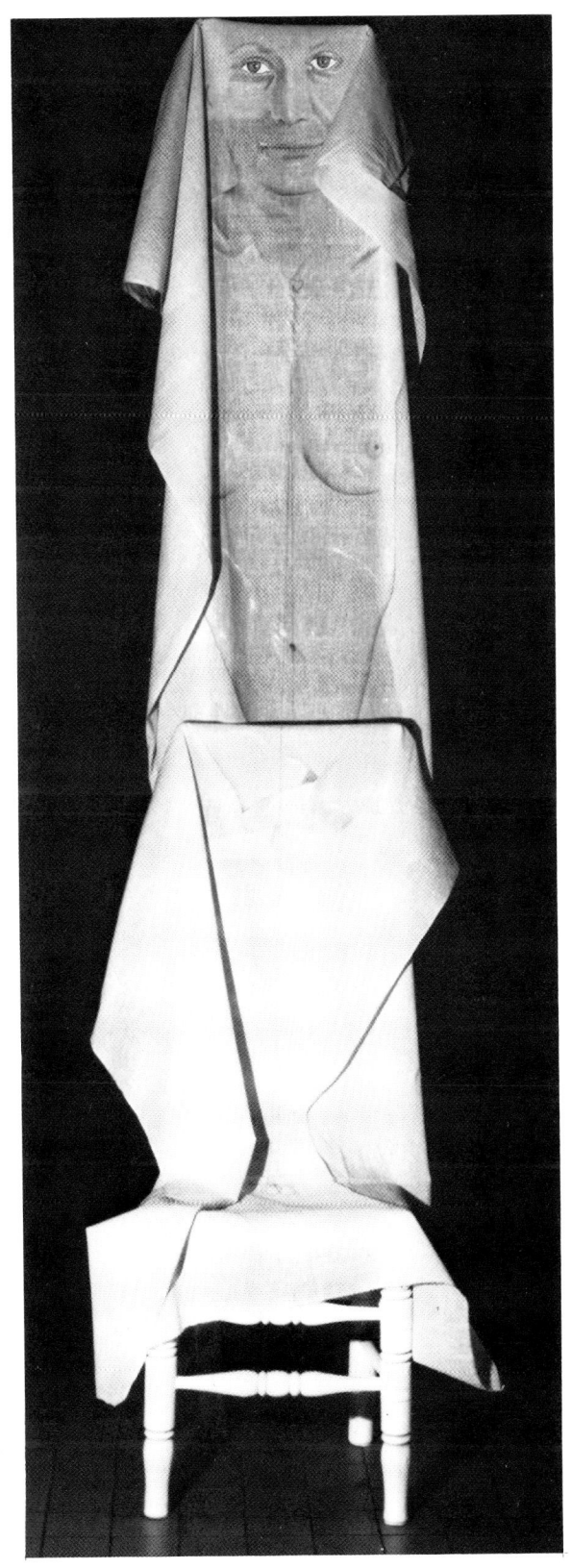

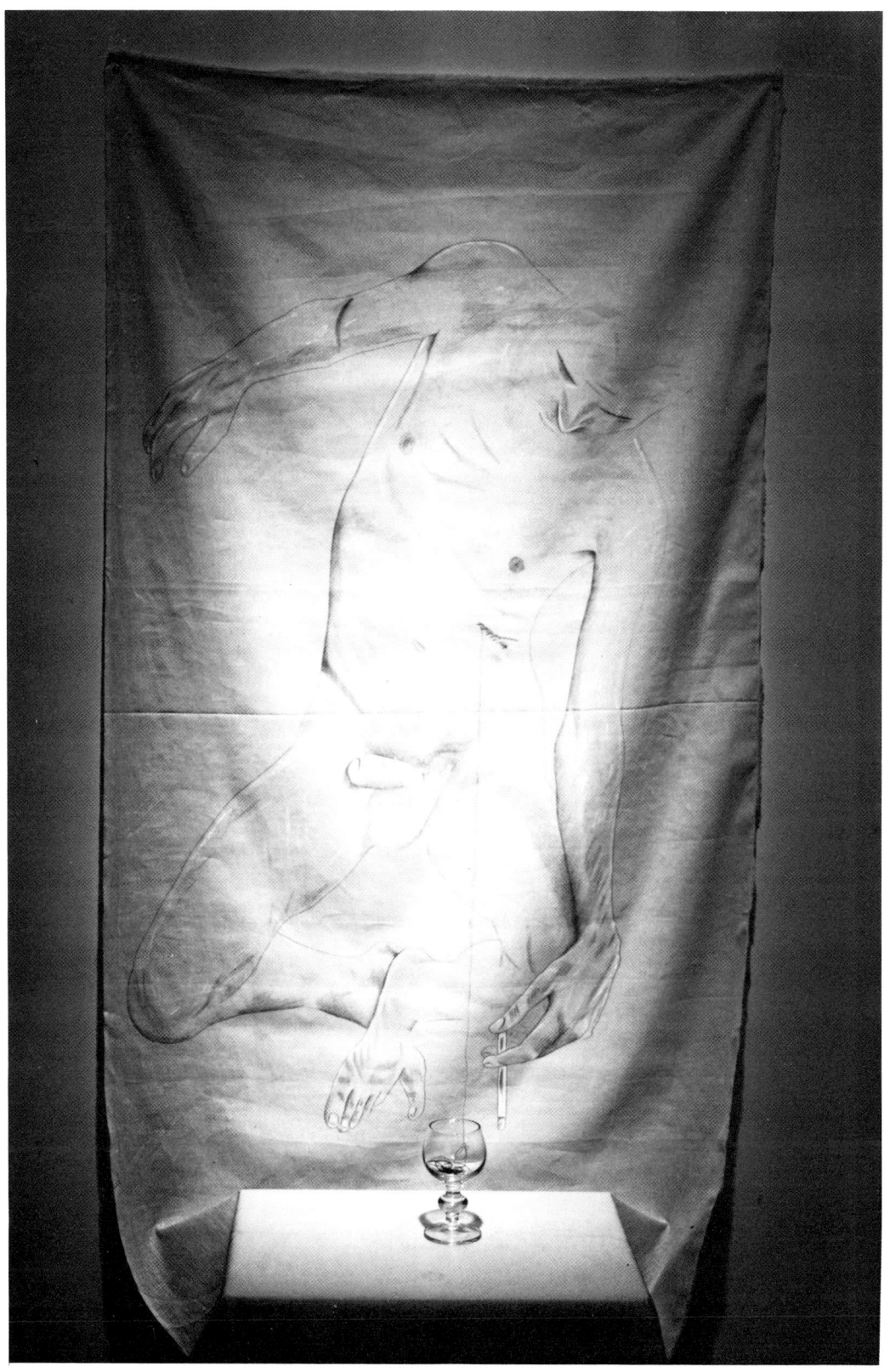

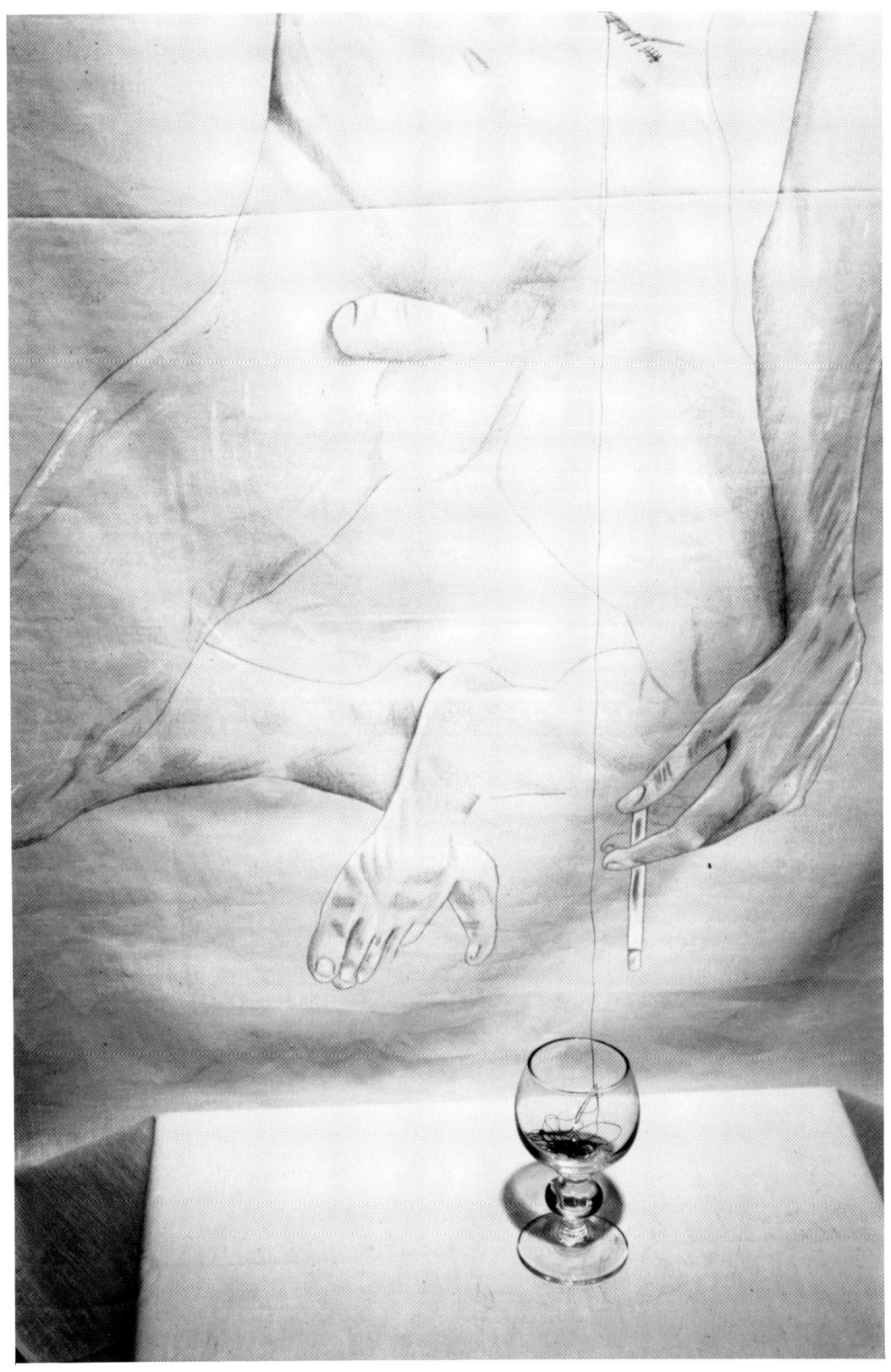

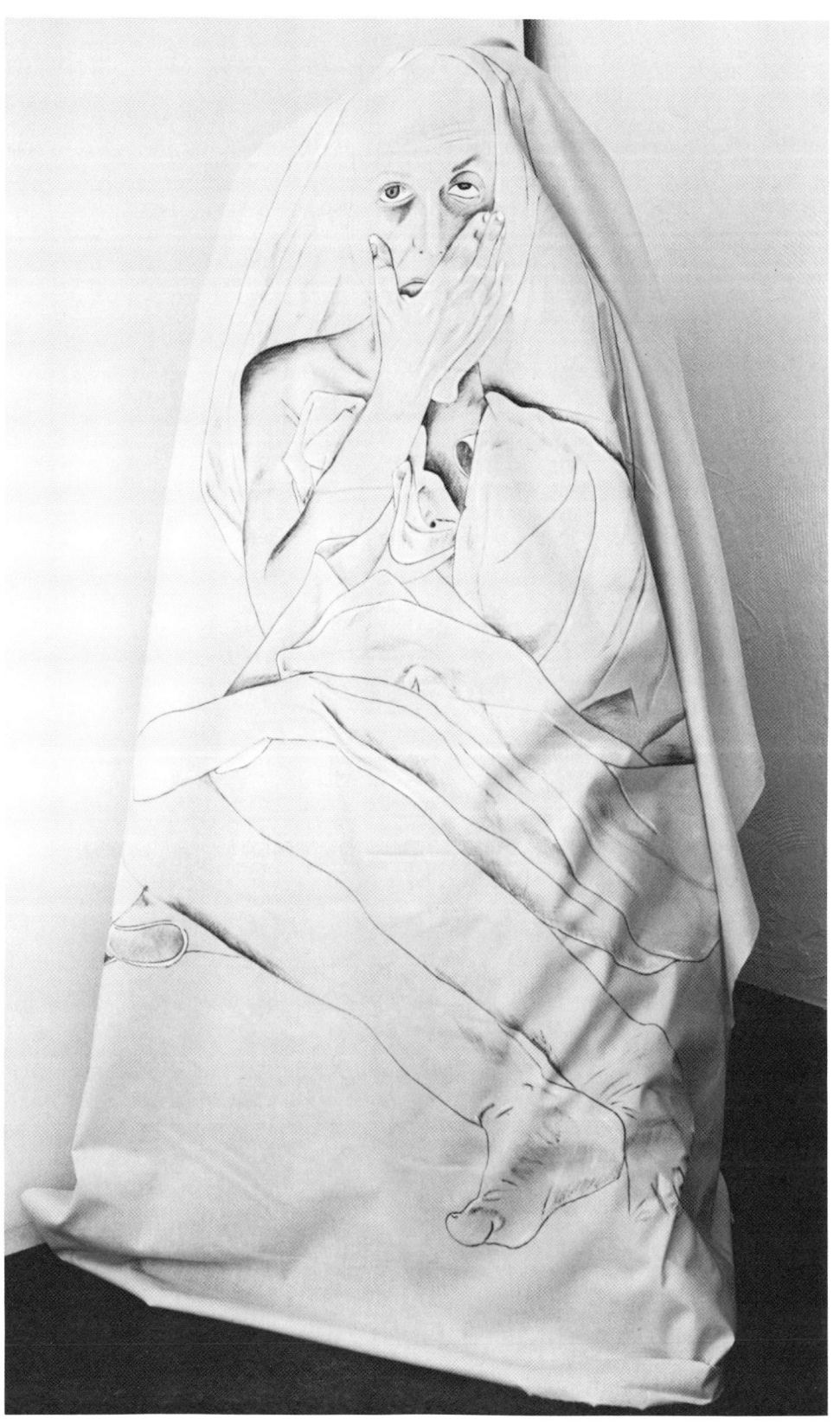

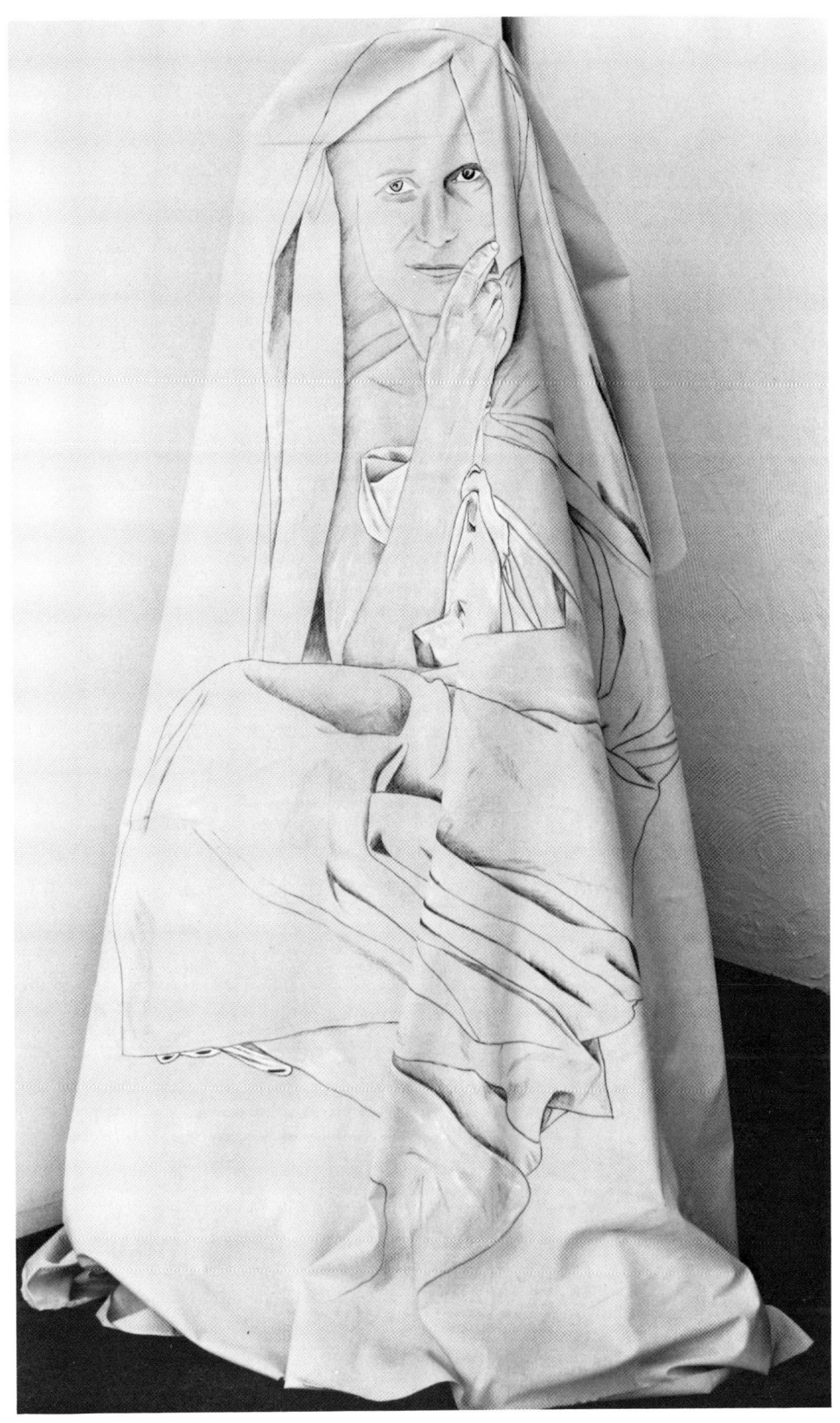

Body Book

1979

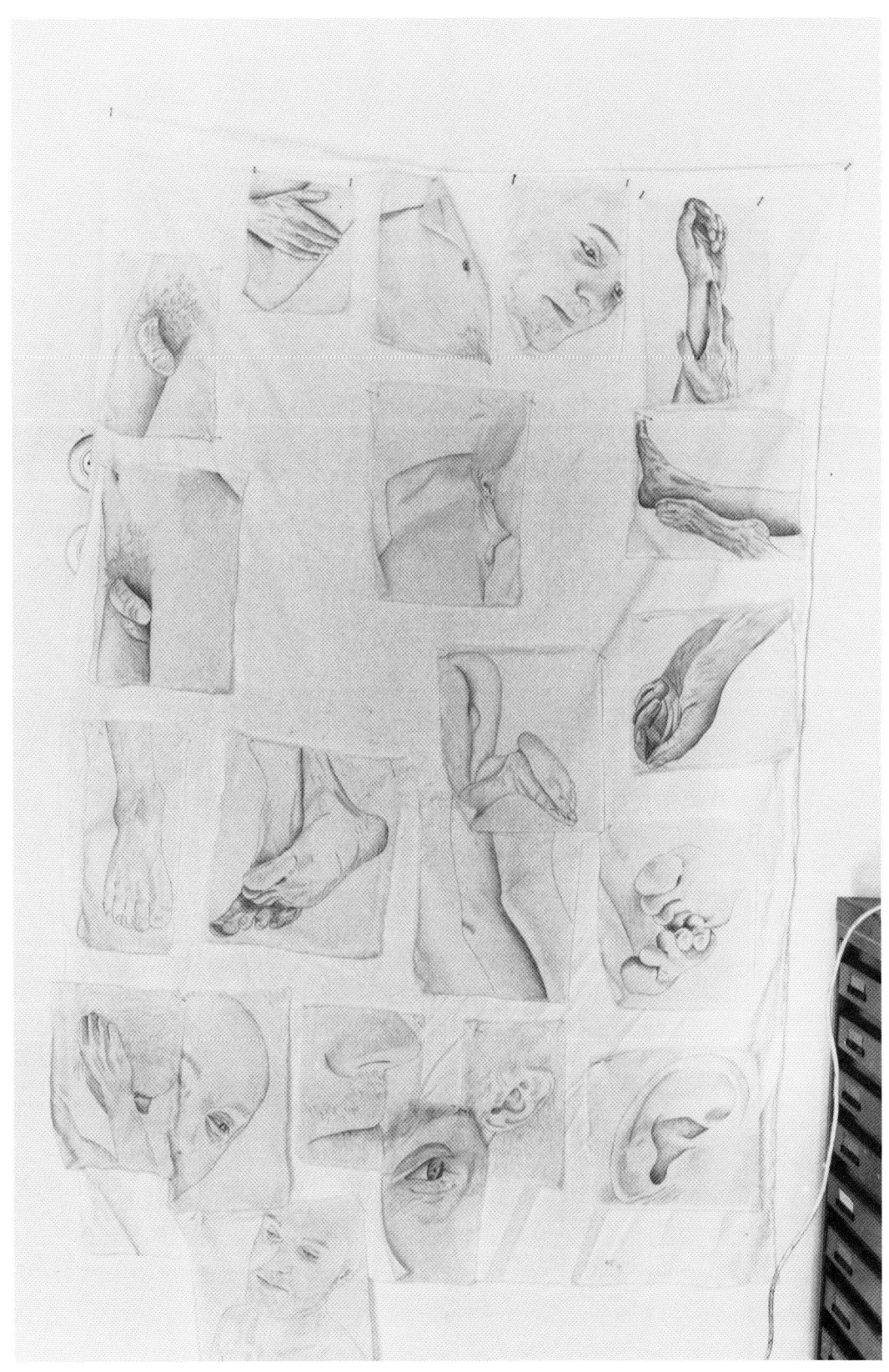

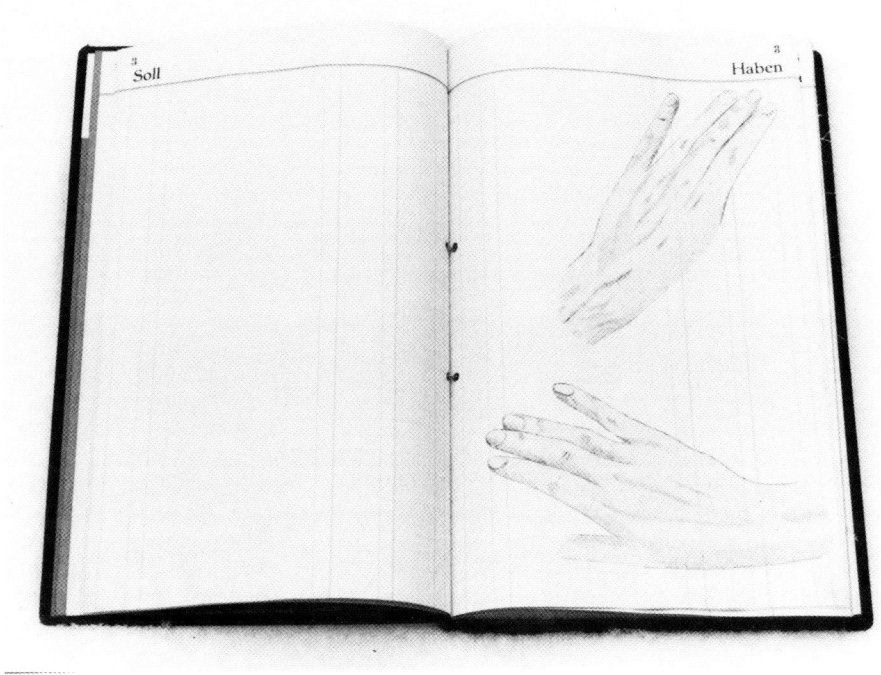

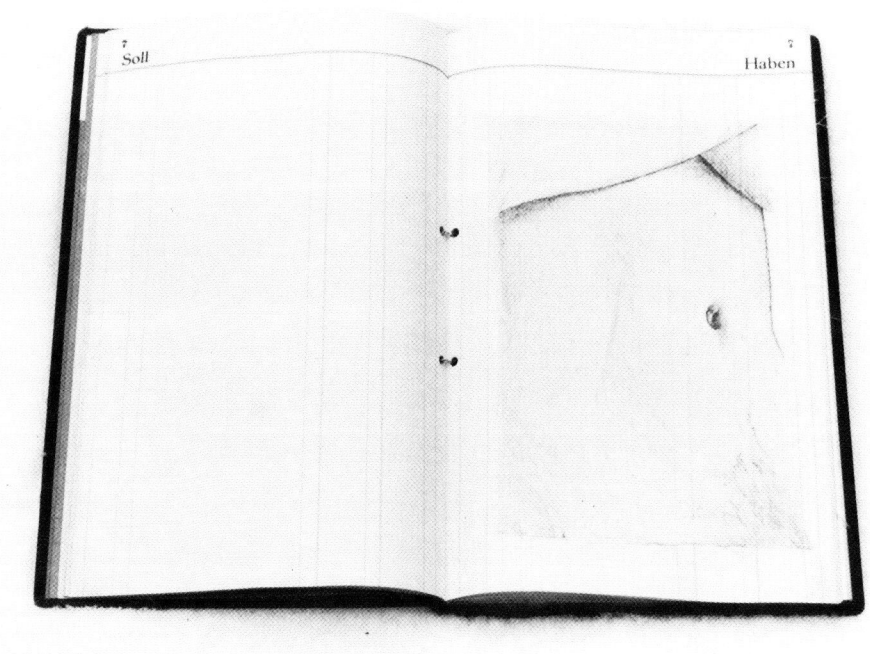

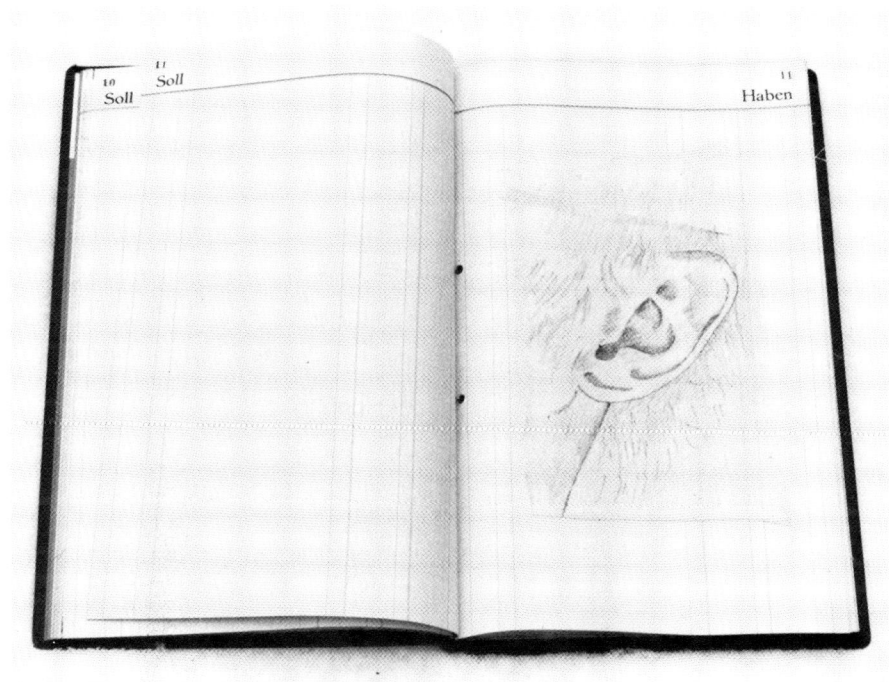

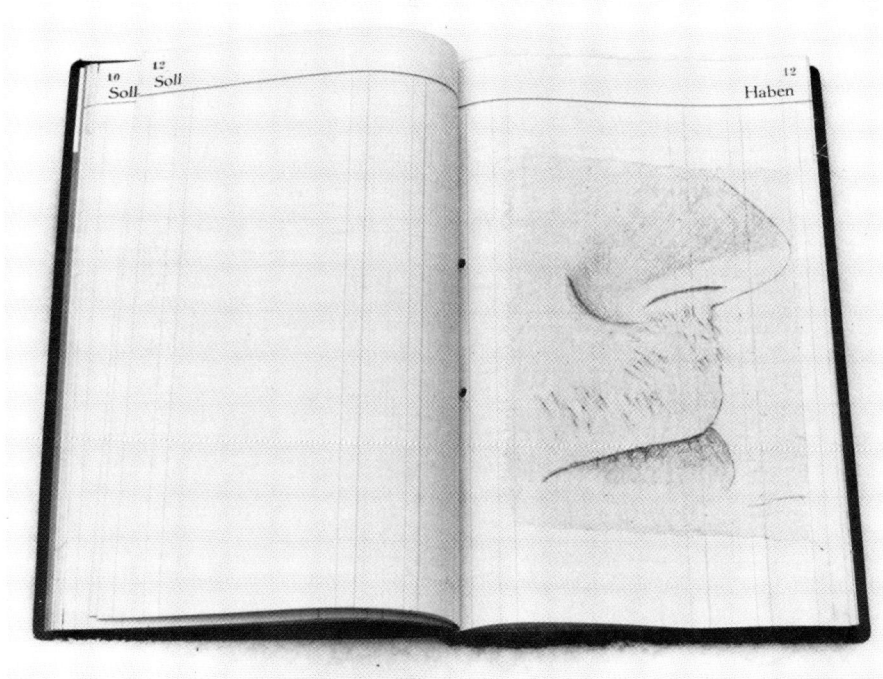

Chairs and Shrouds

1981–1986

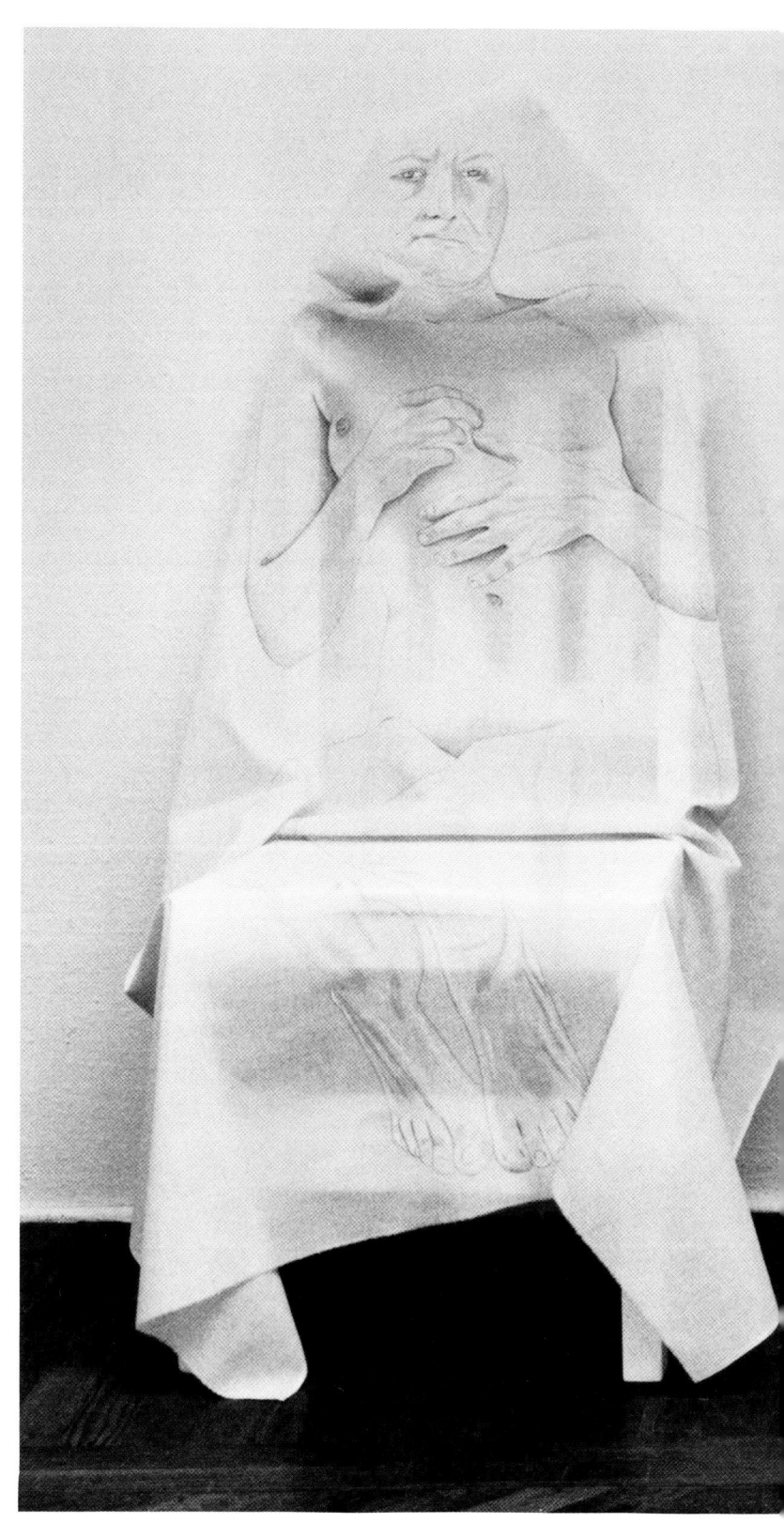

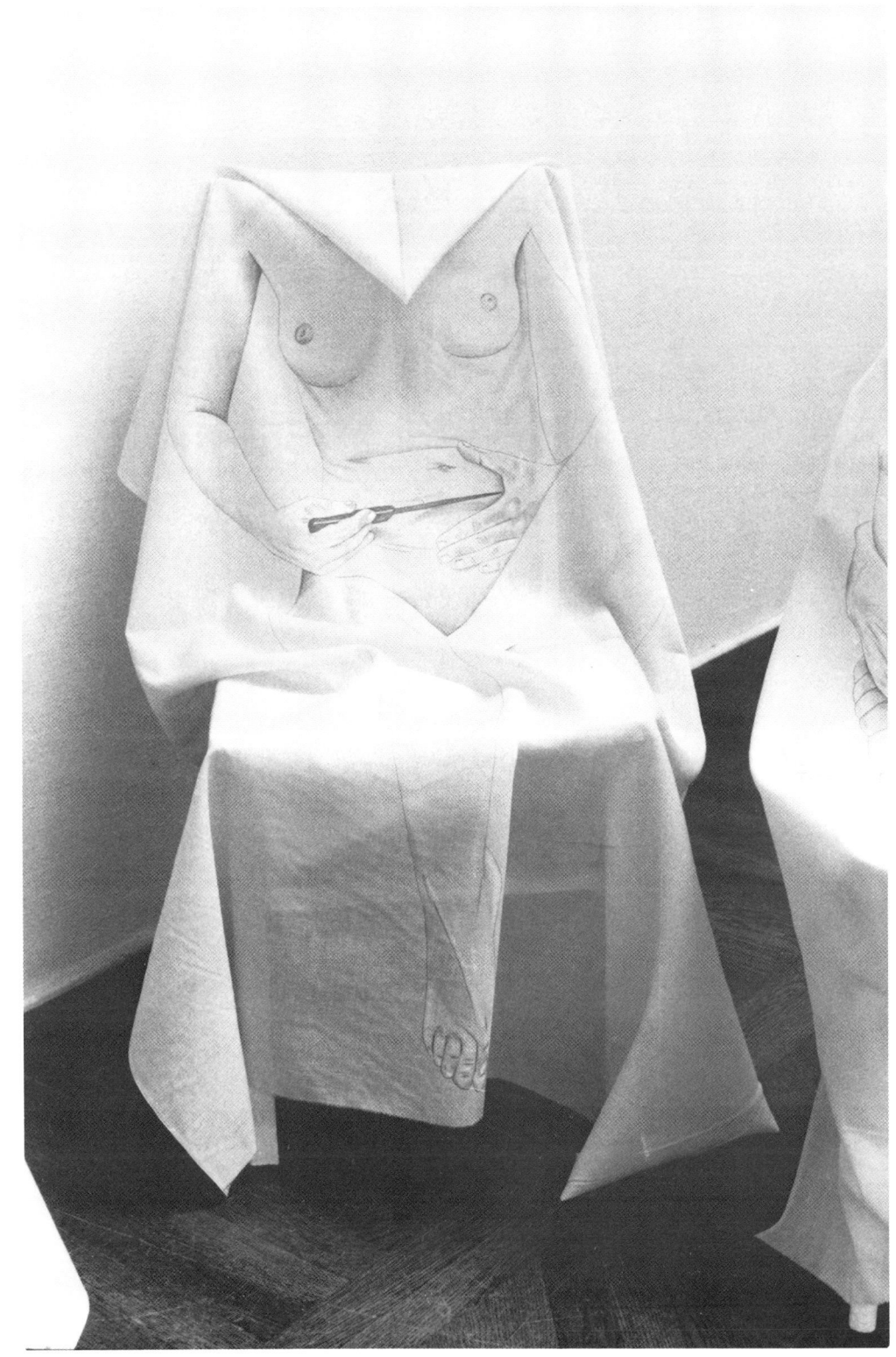

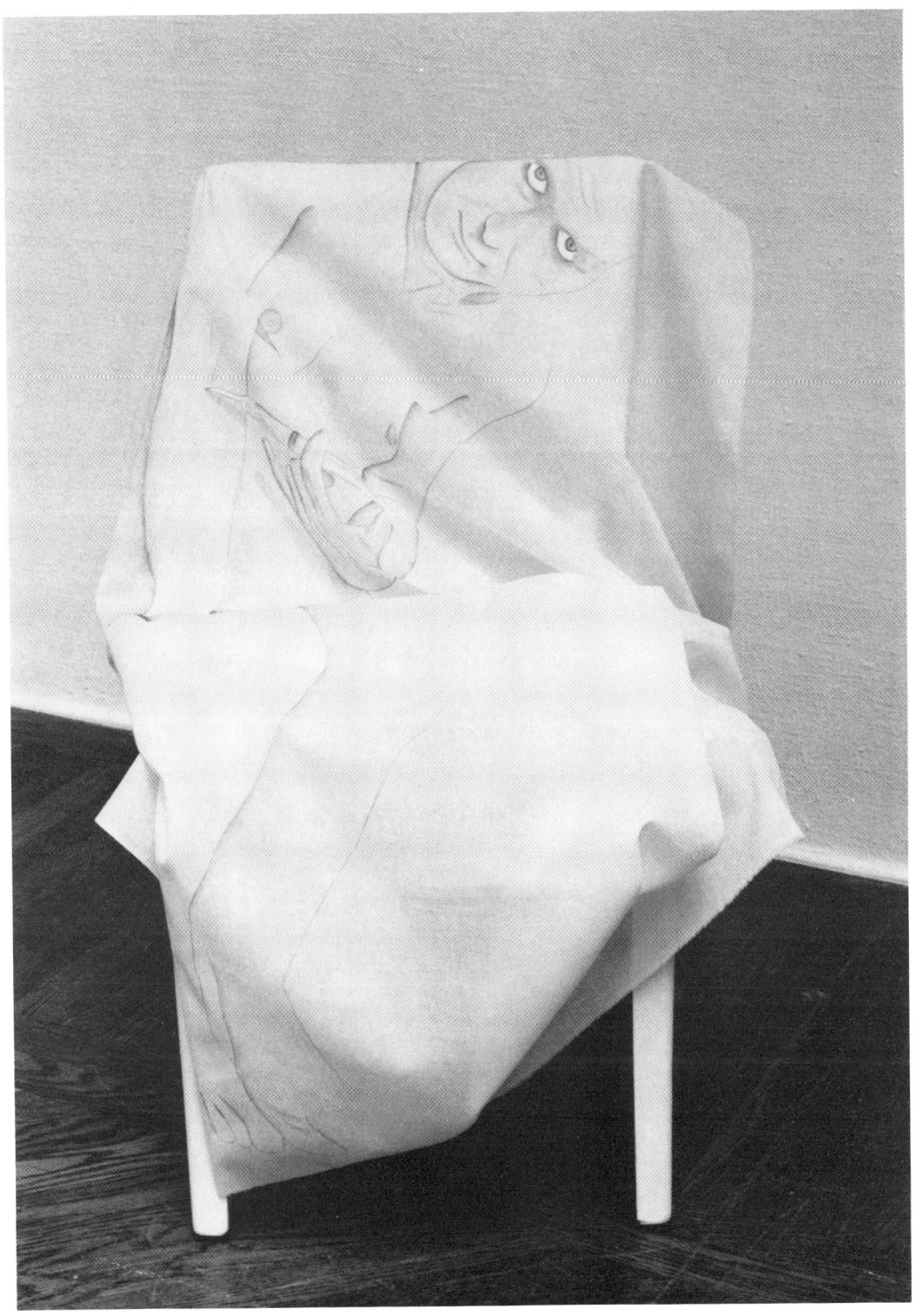

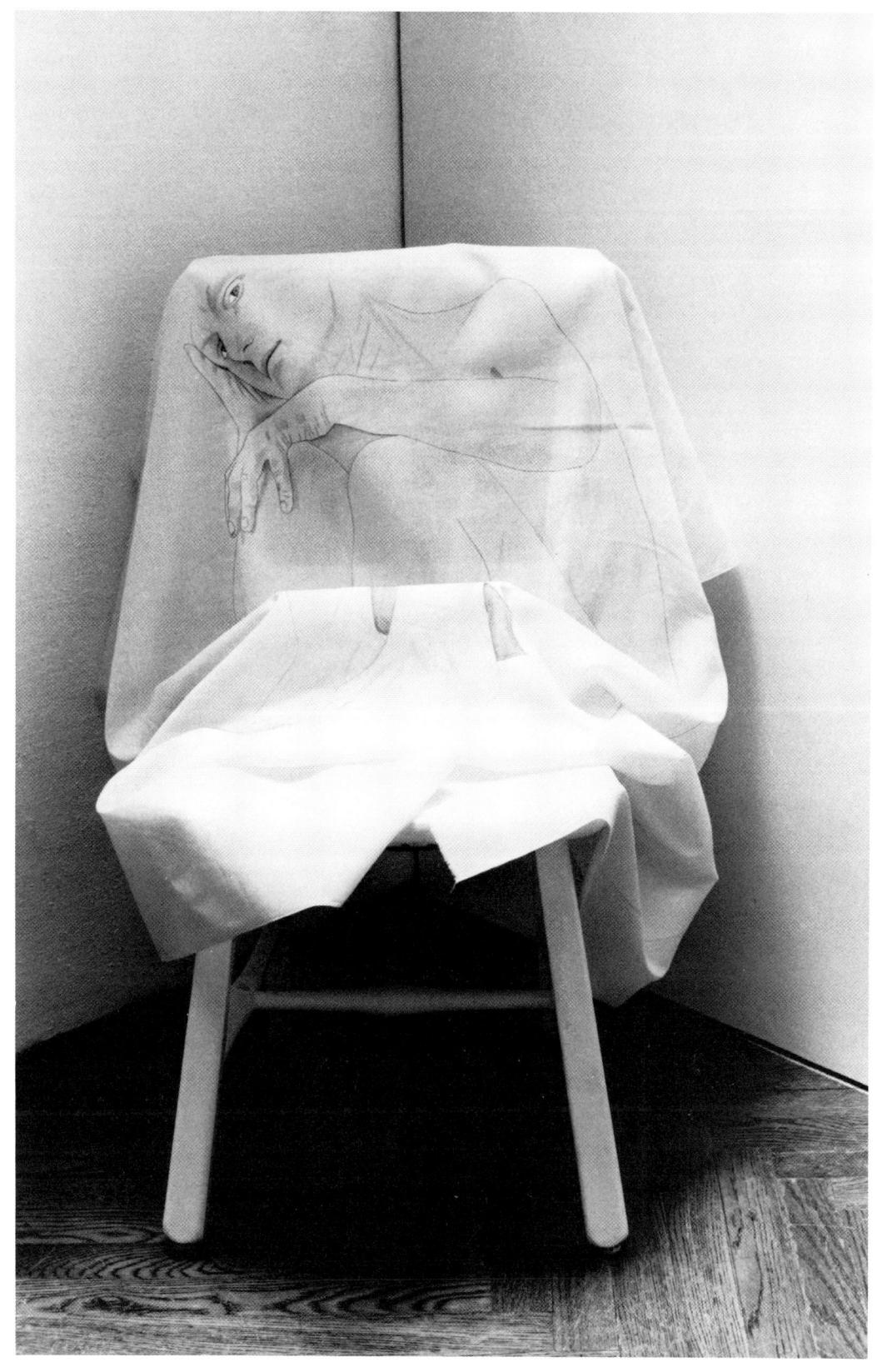

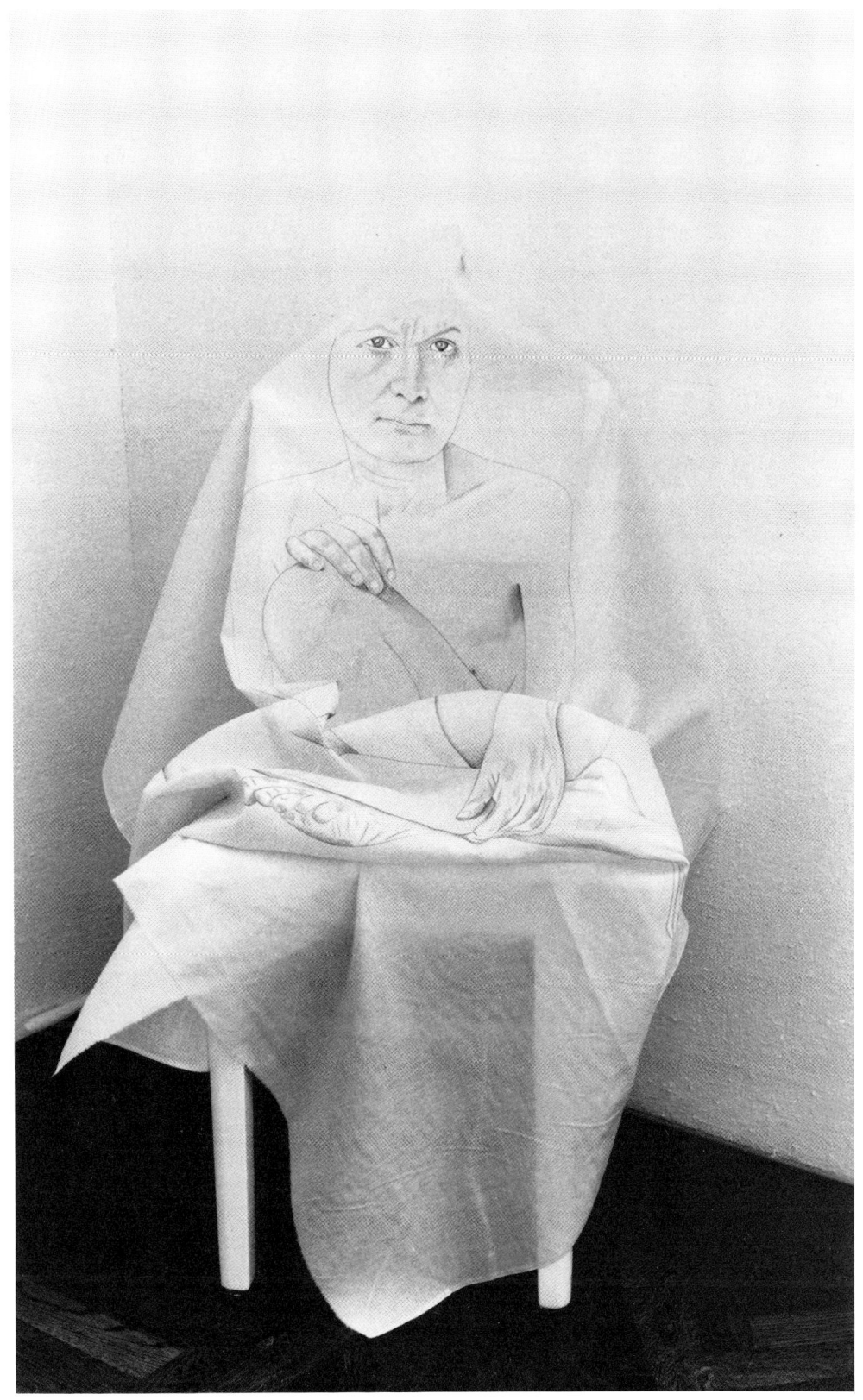

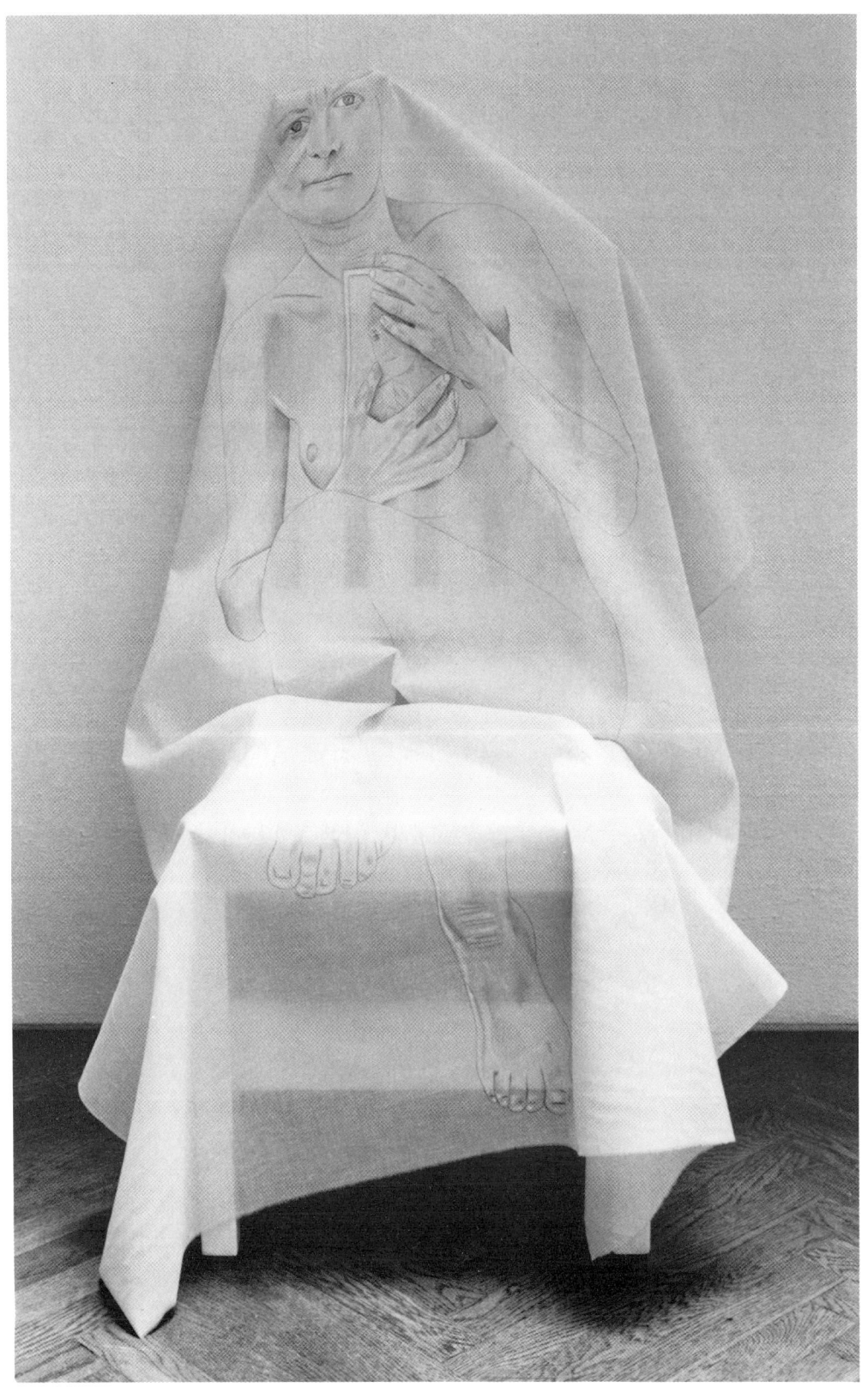

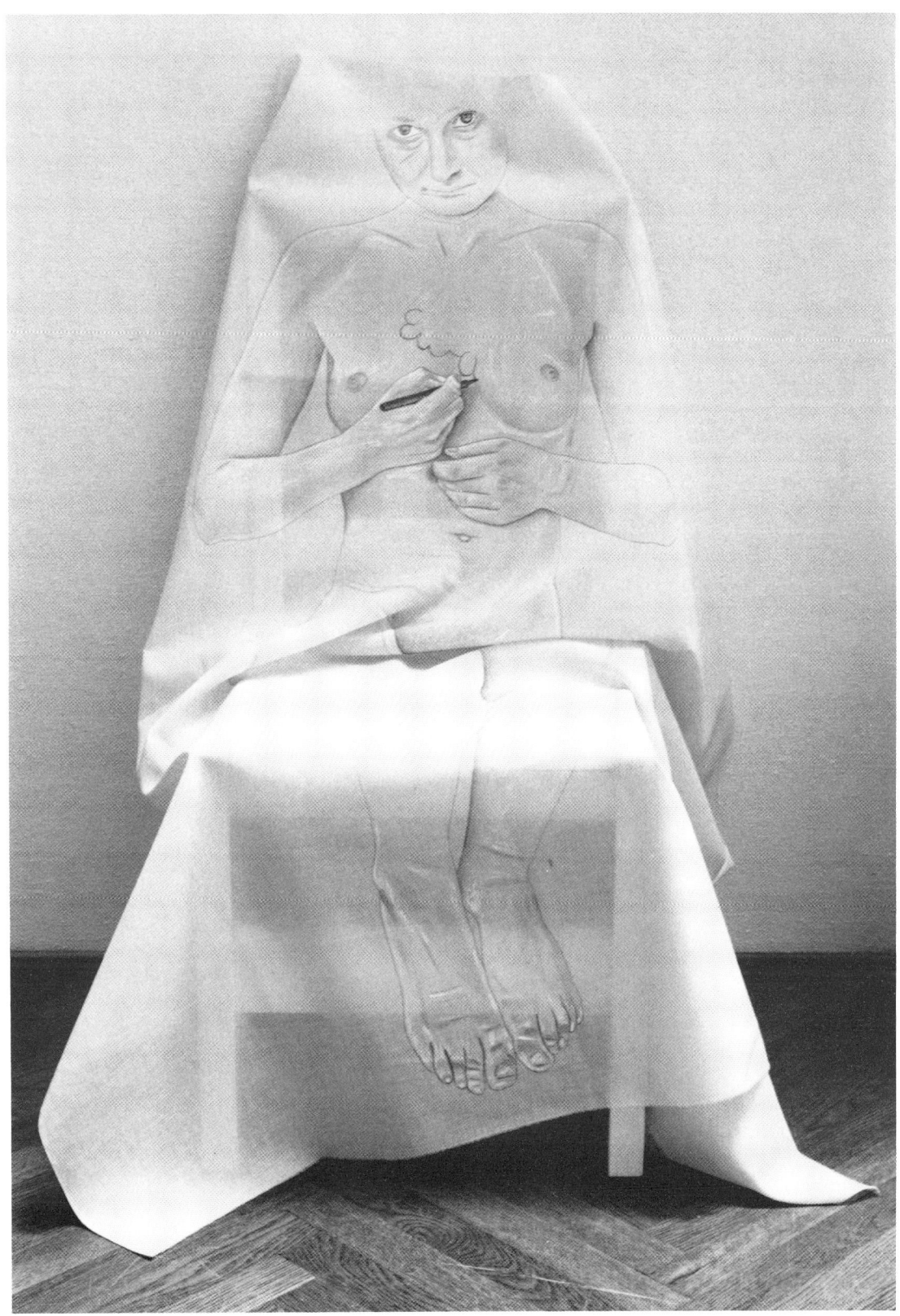

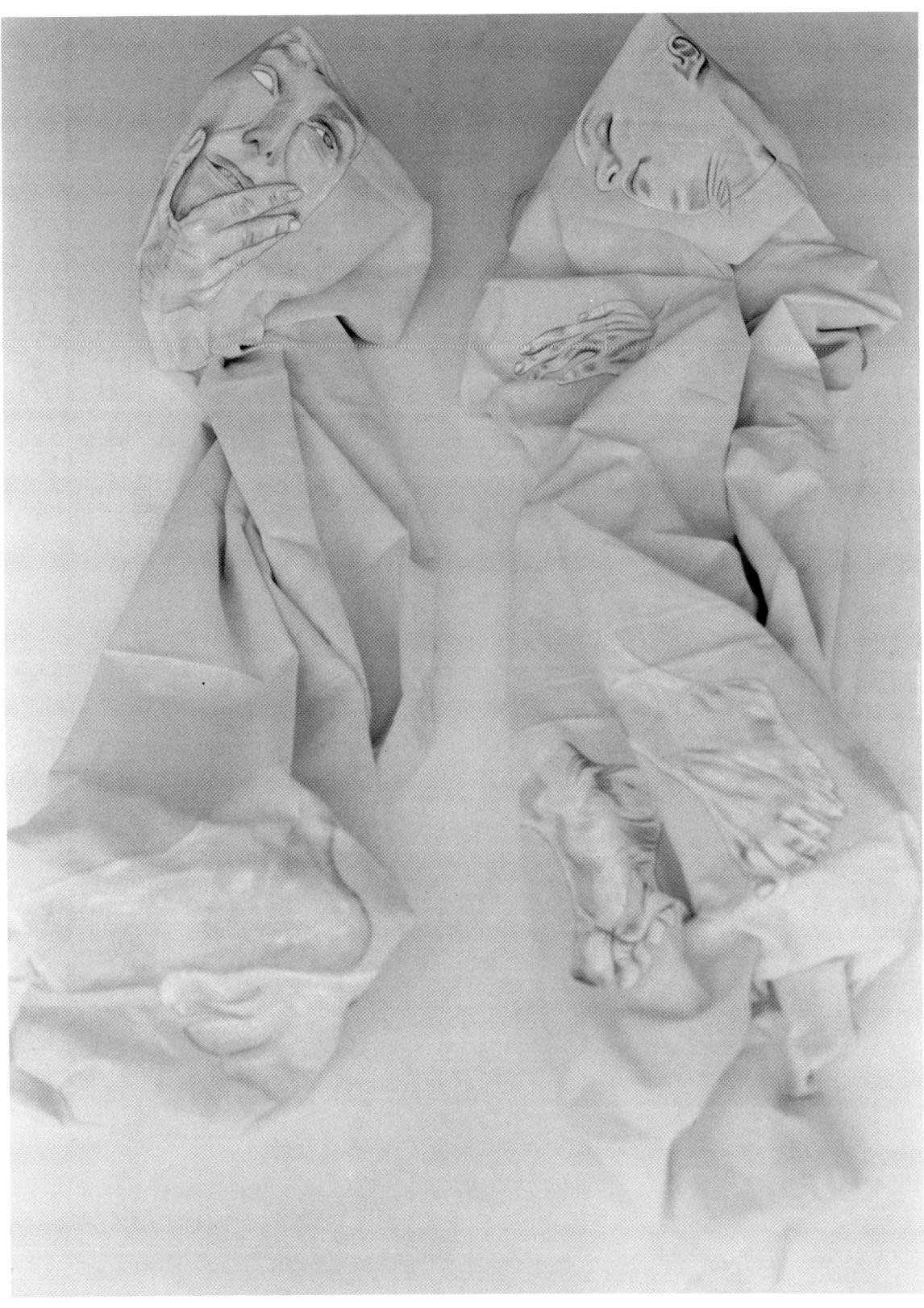

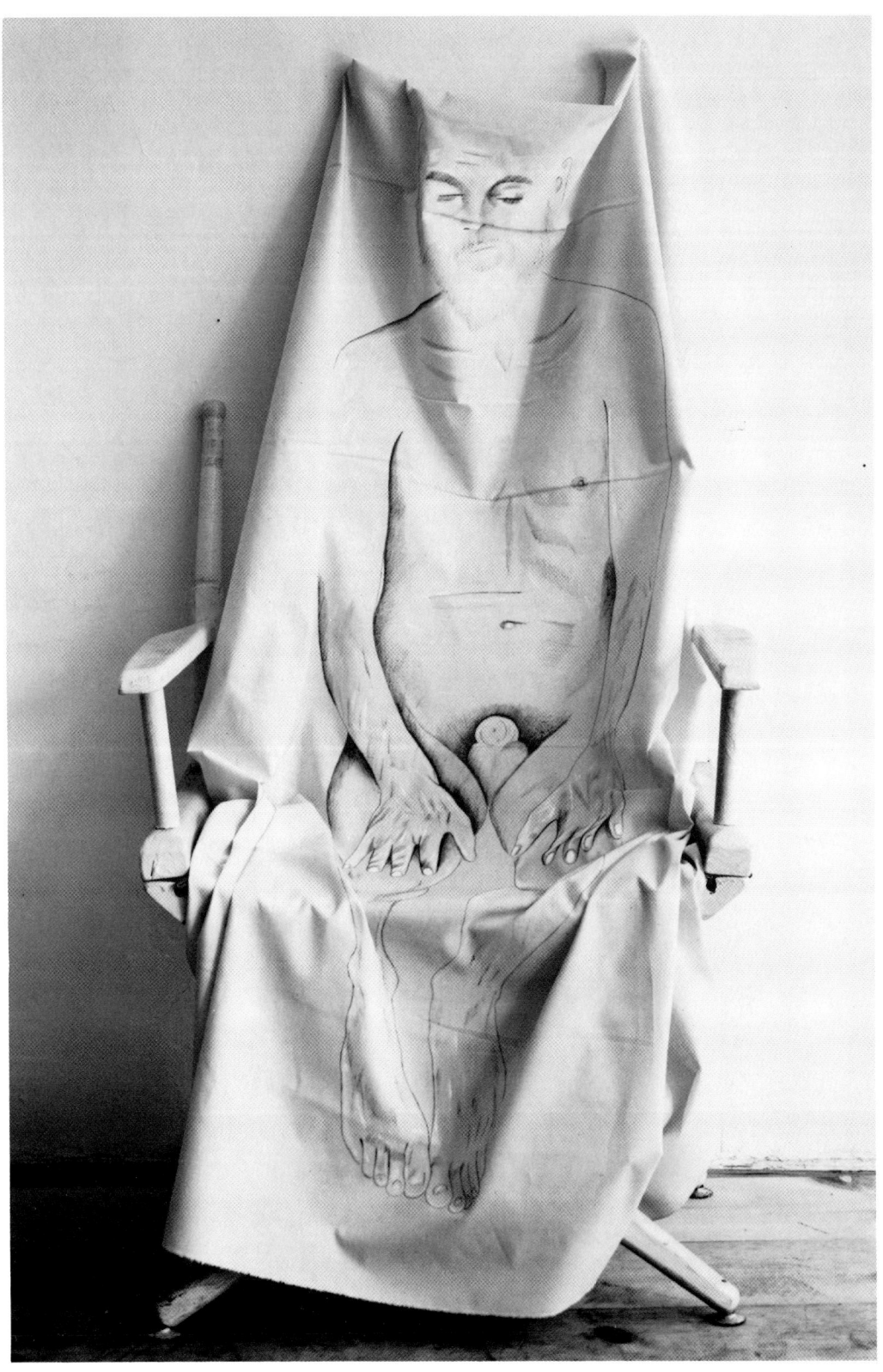

Outdoor Installations

1984–1986

Princeton: In the Backyard

1985

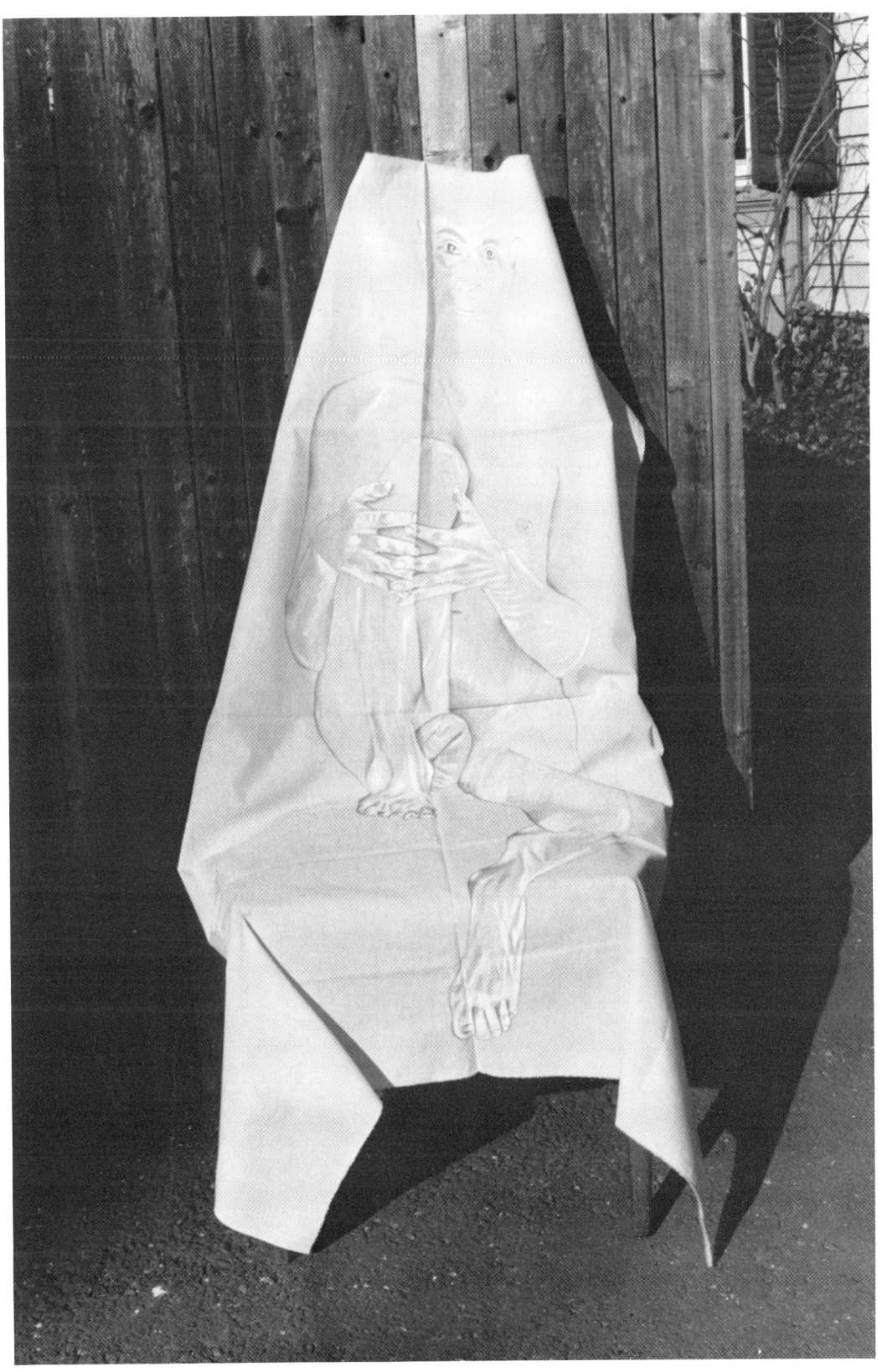

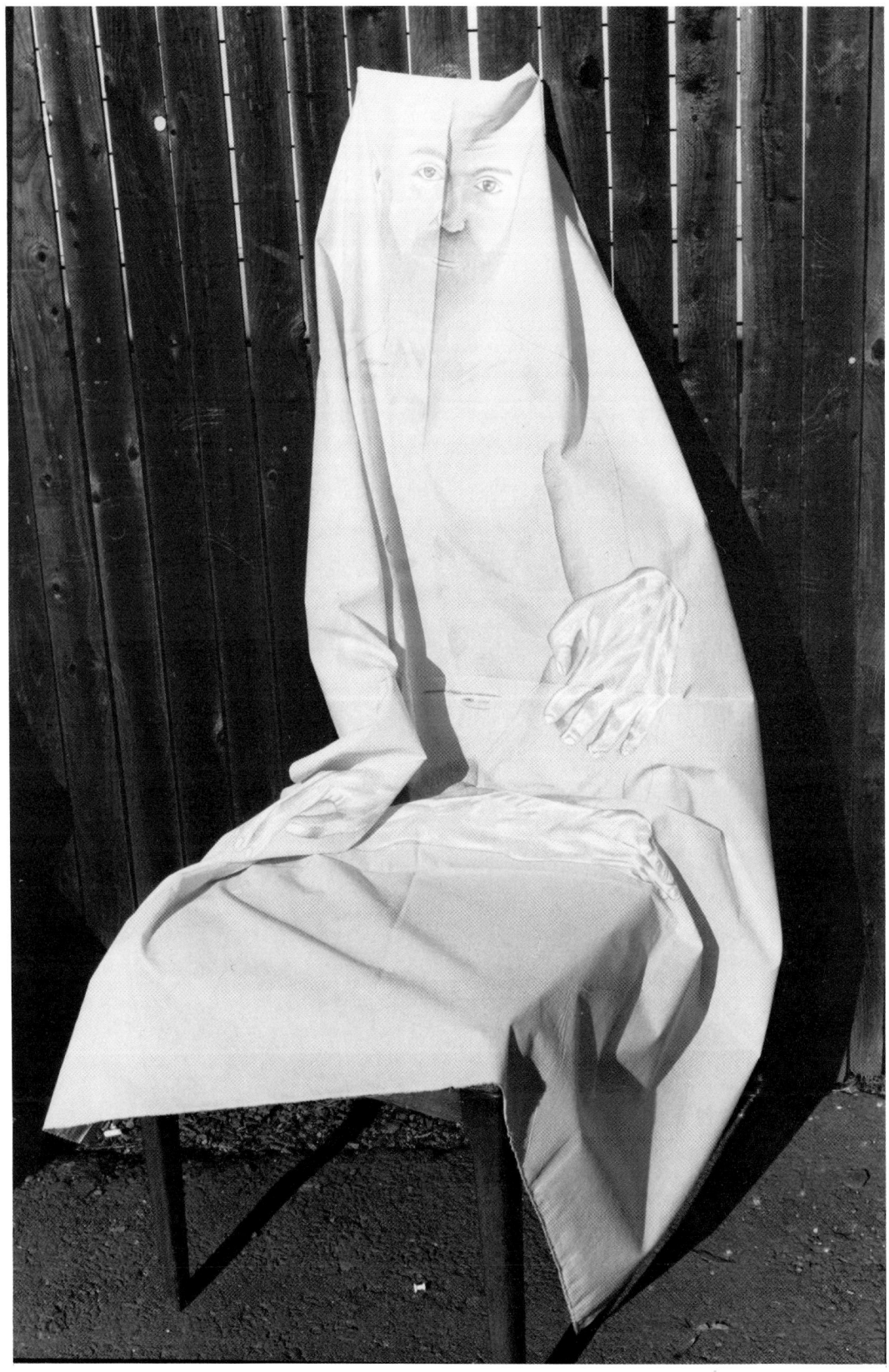

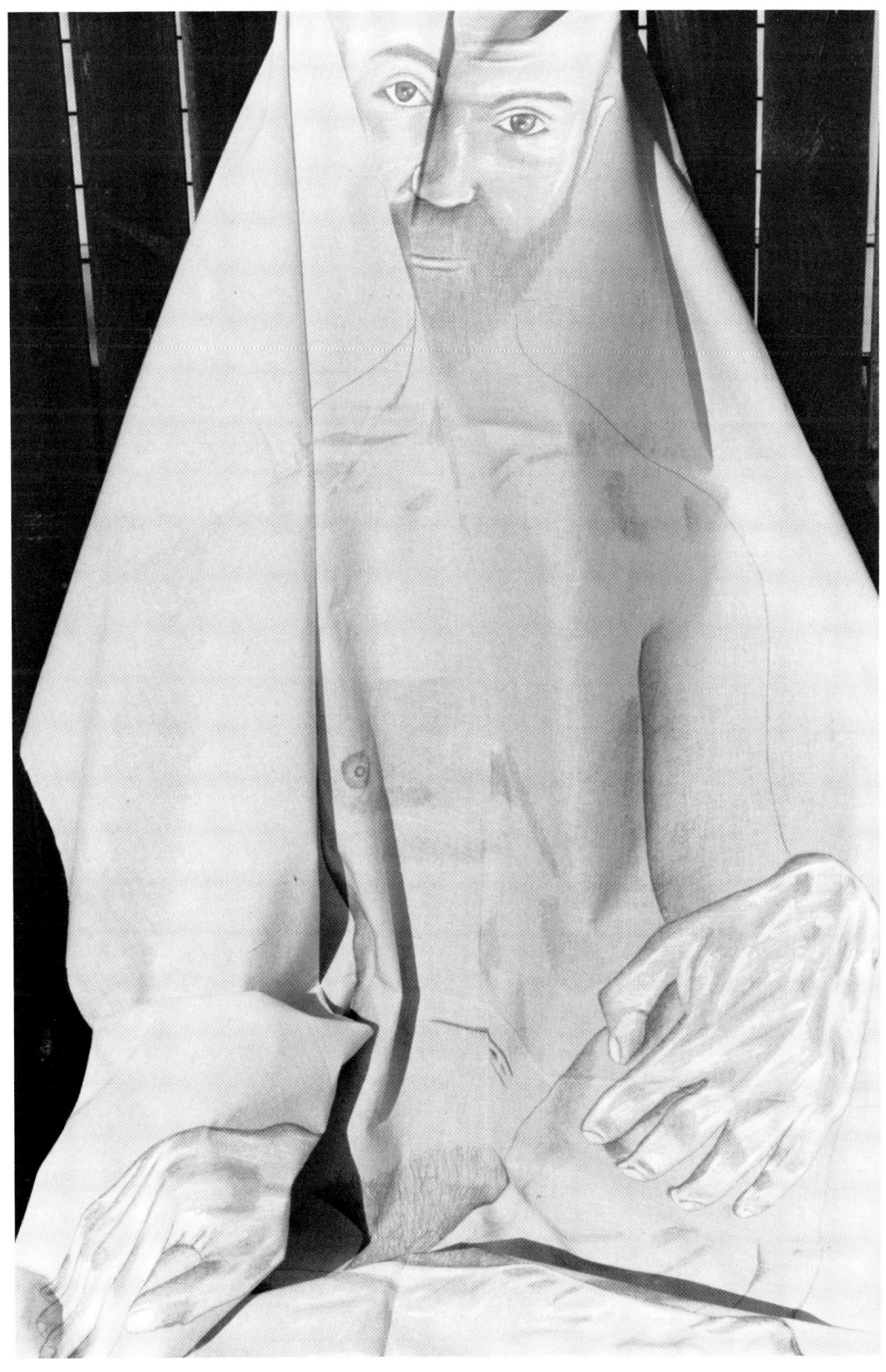

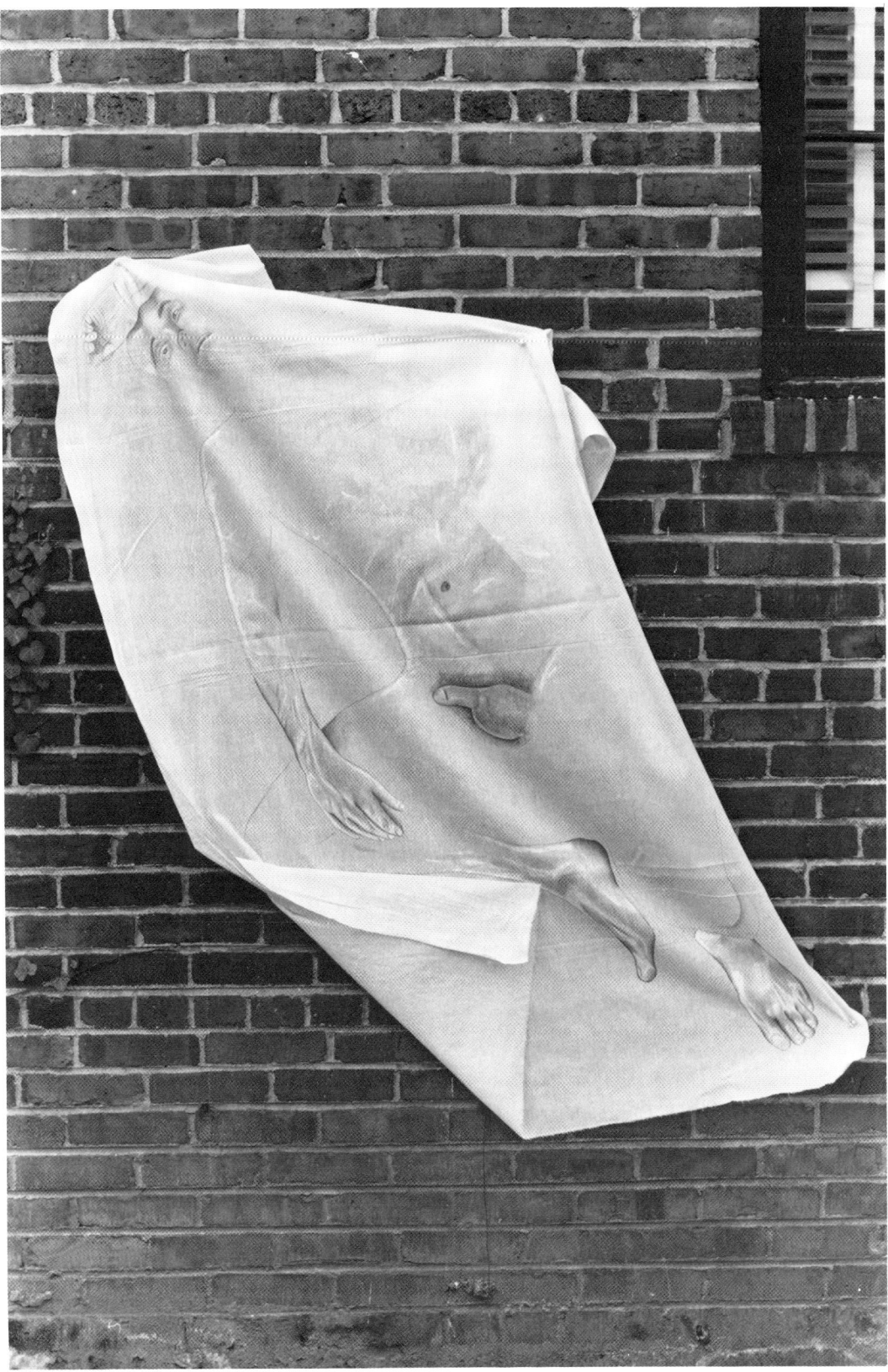

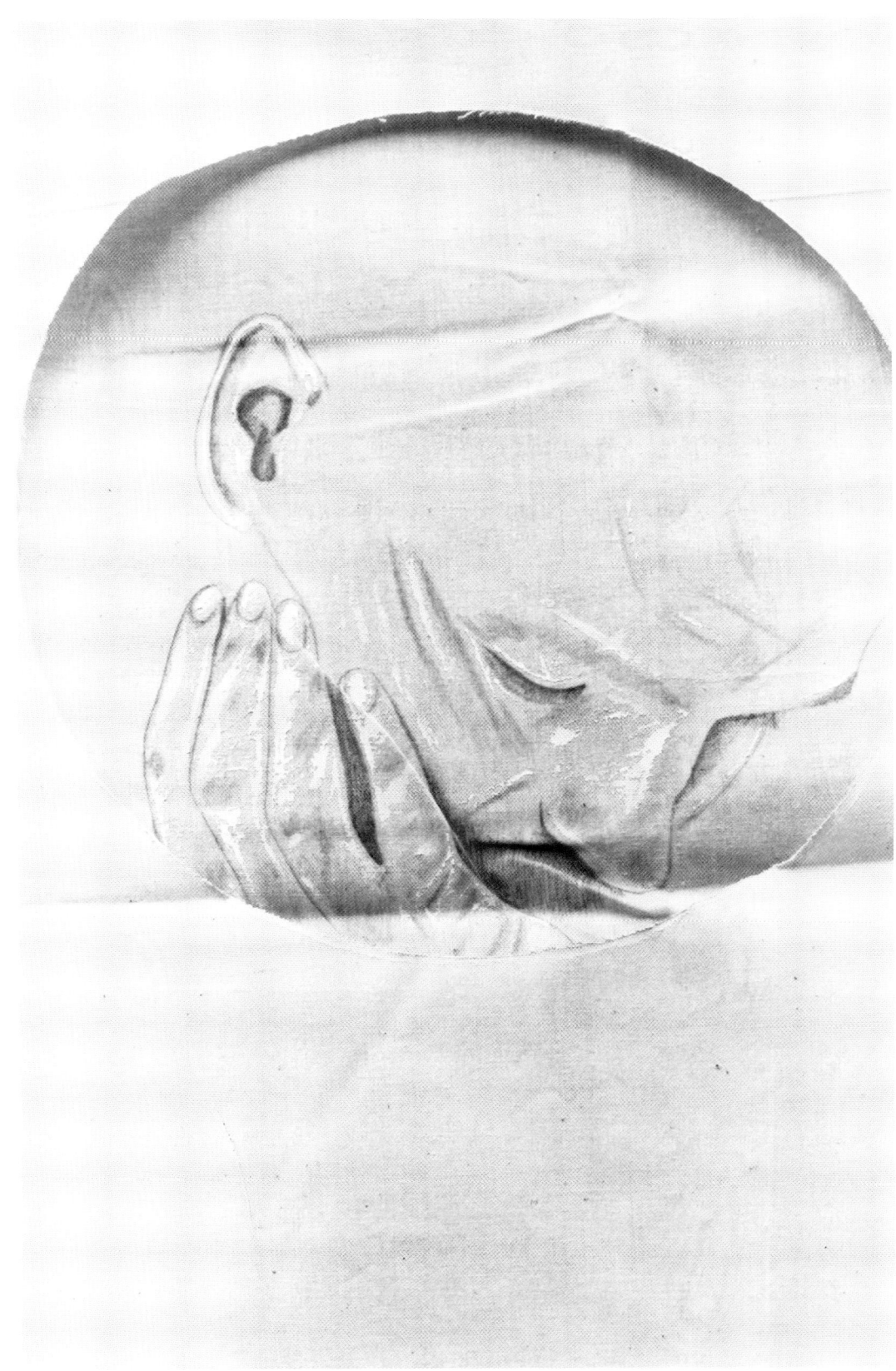

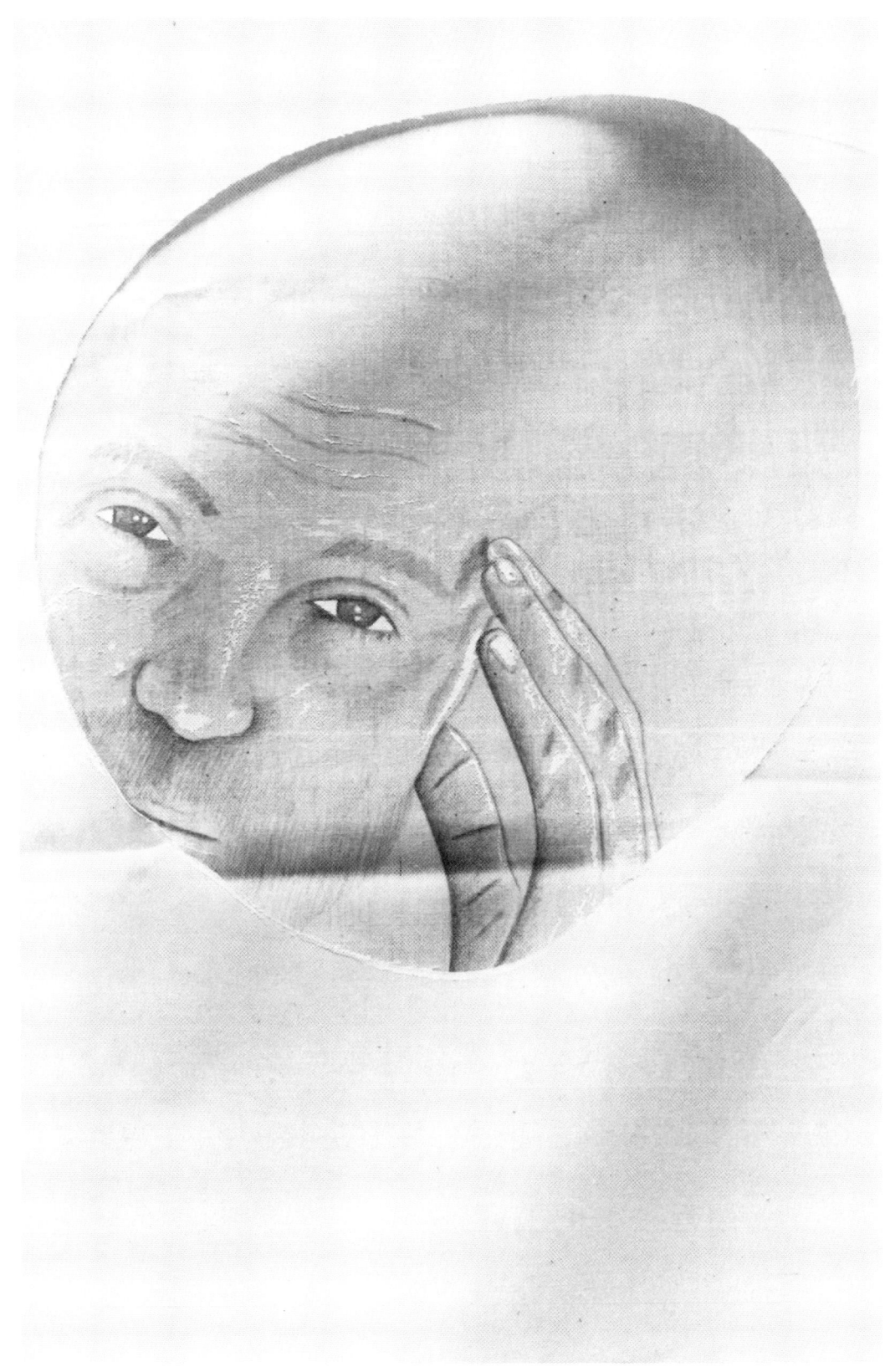

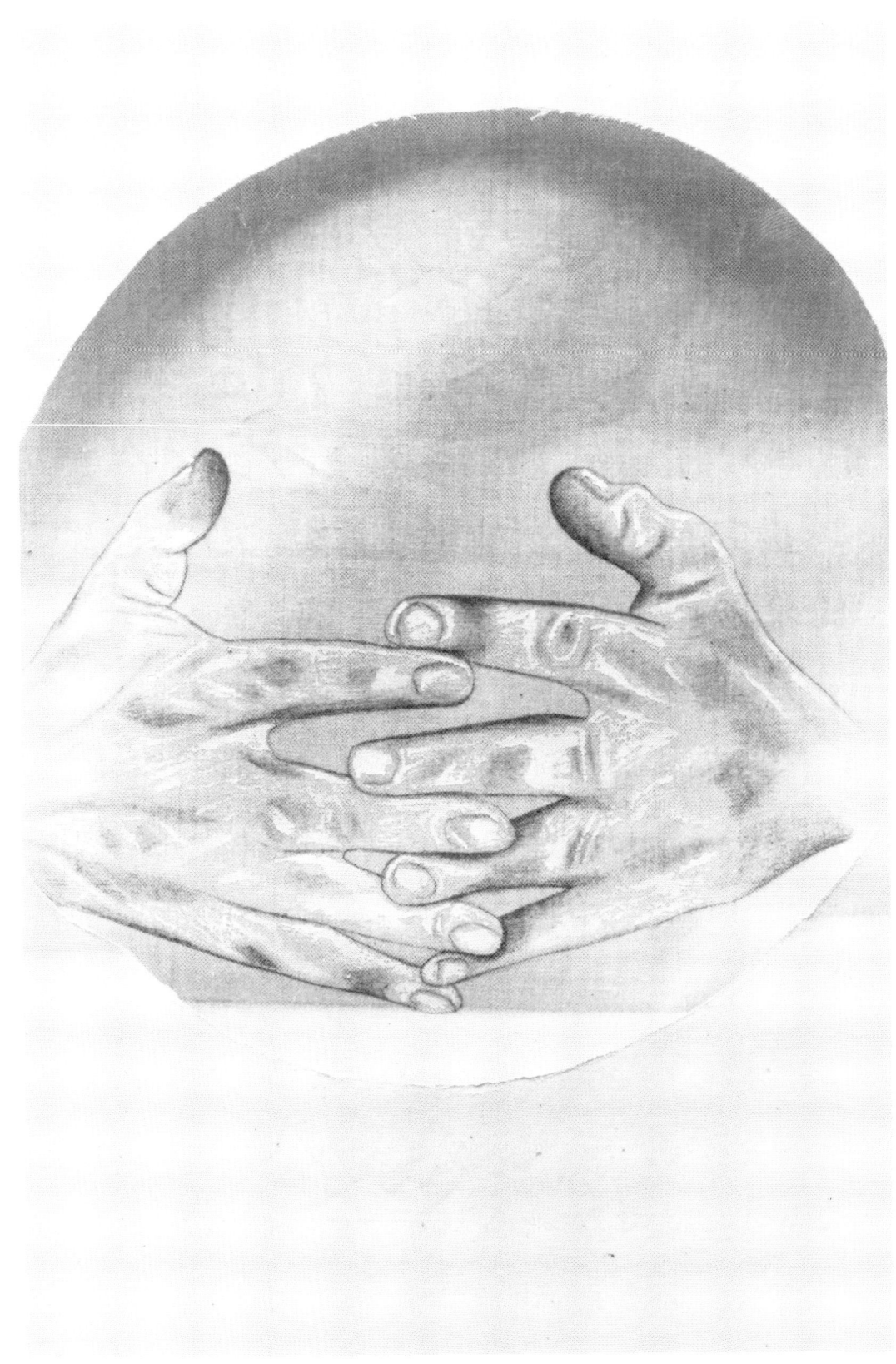

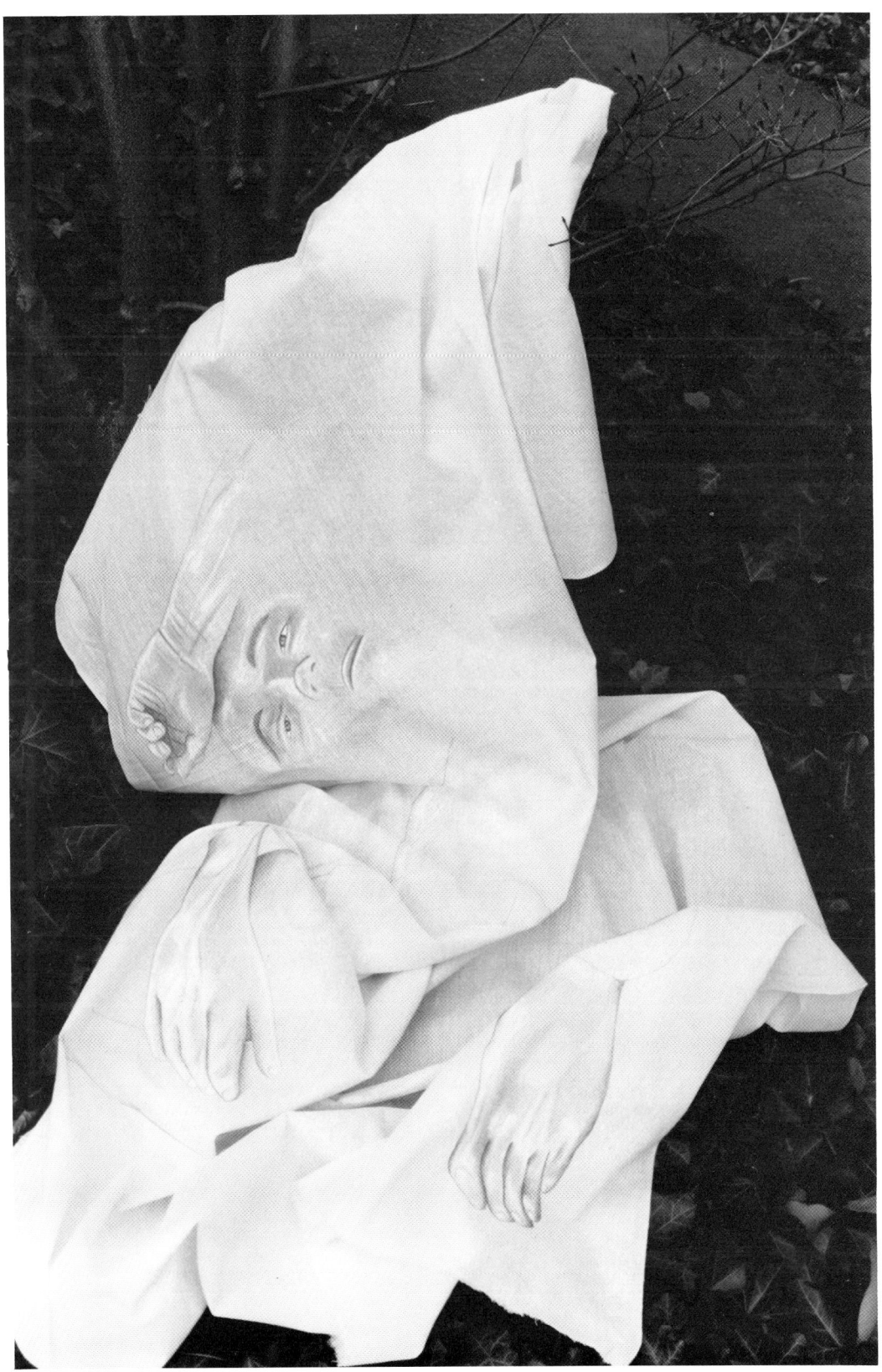

Princeton: Fall and Spring

1984–1985

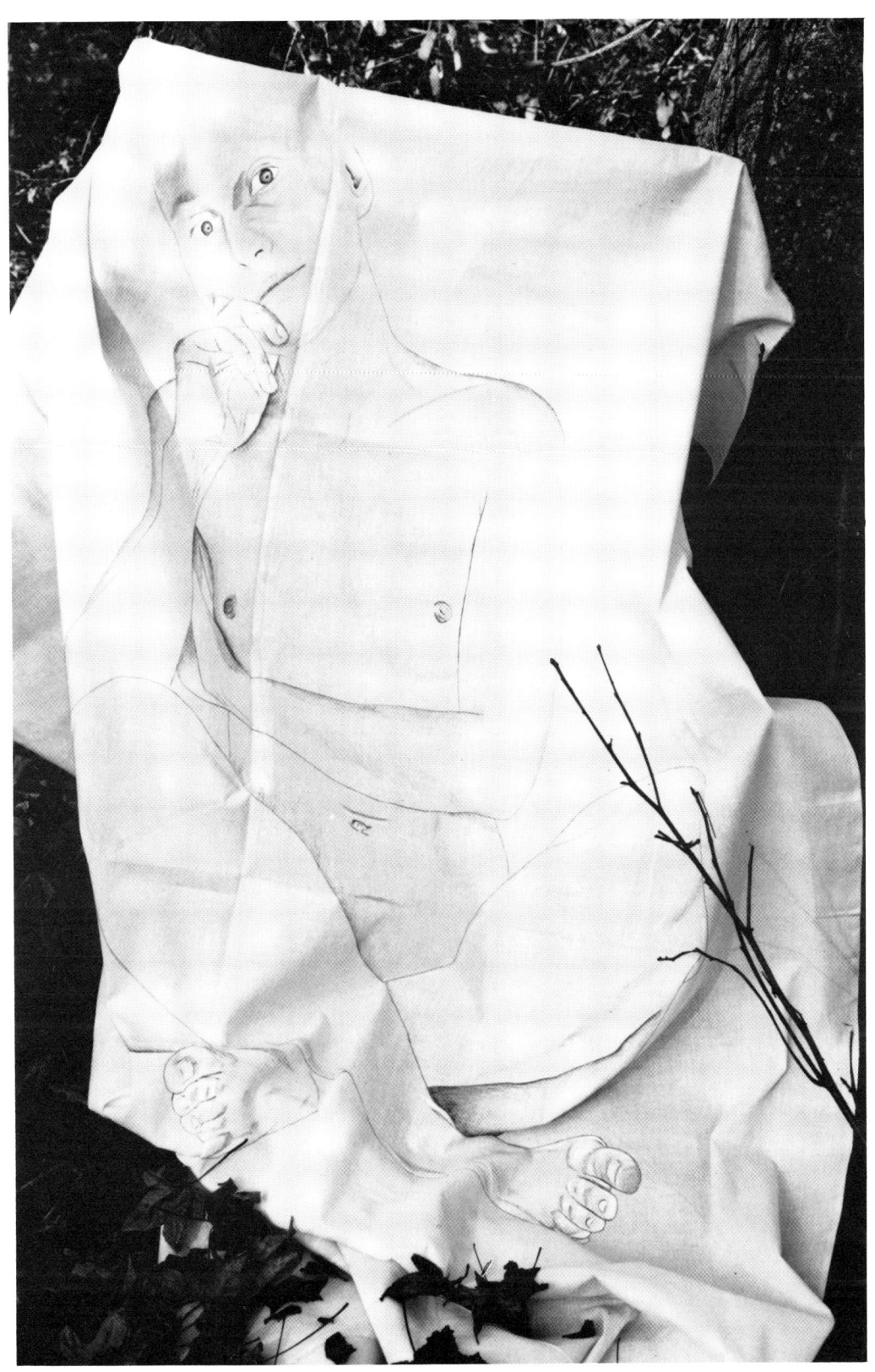

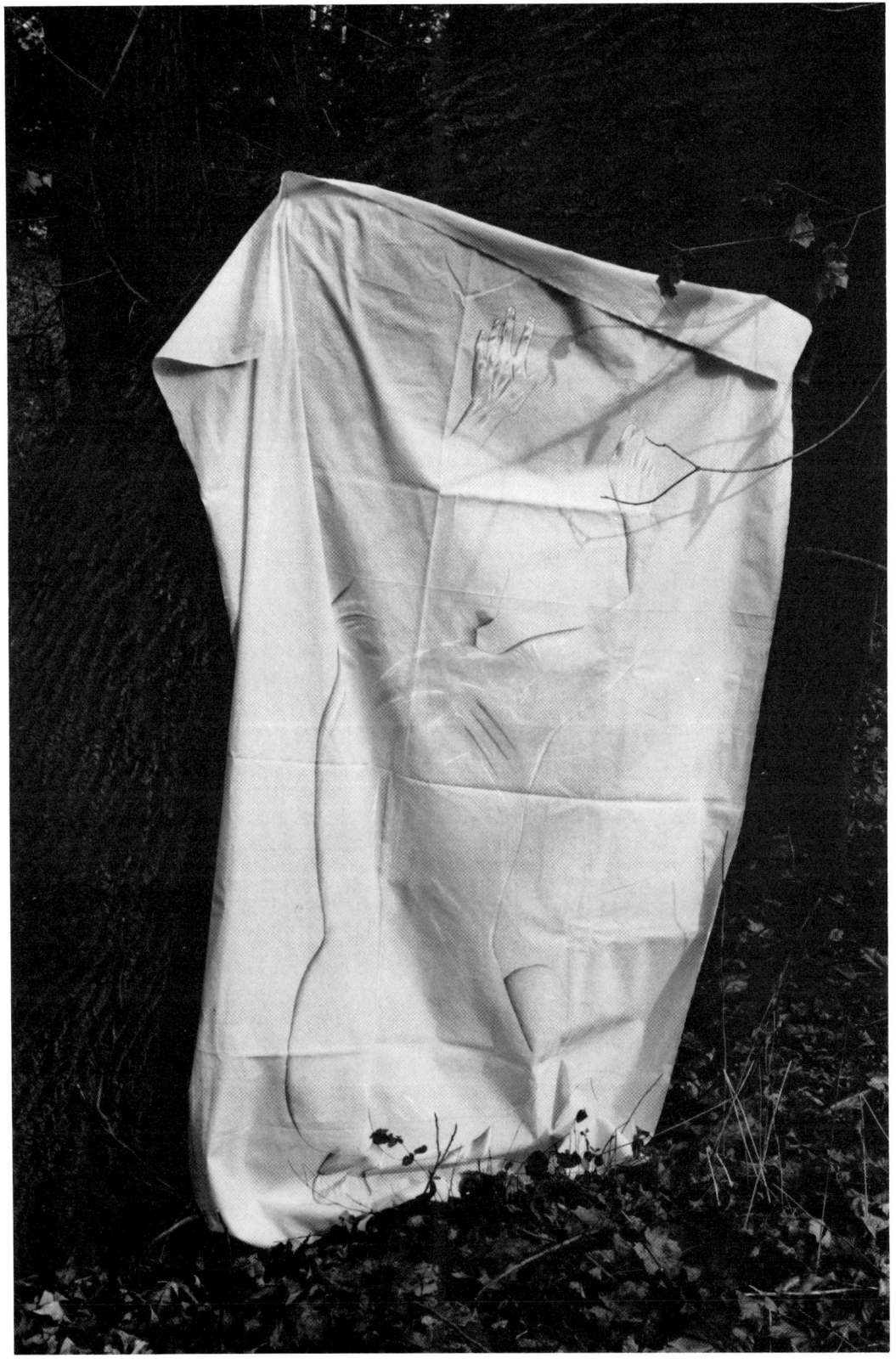

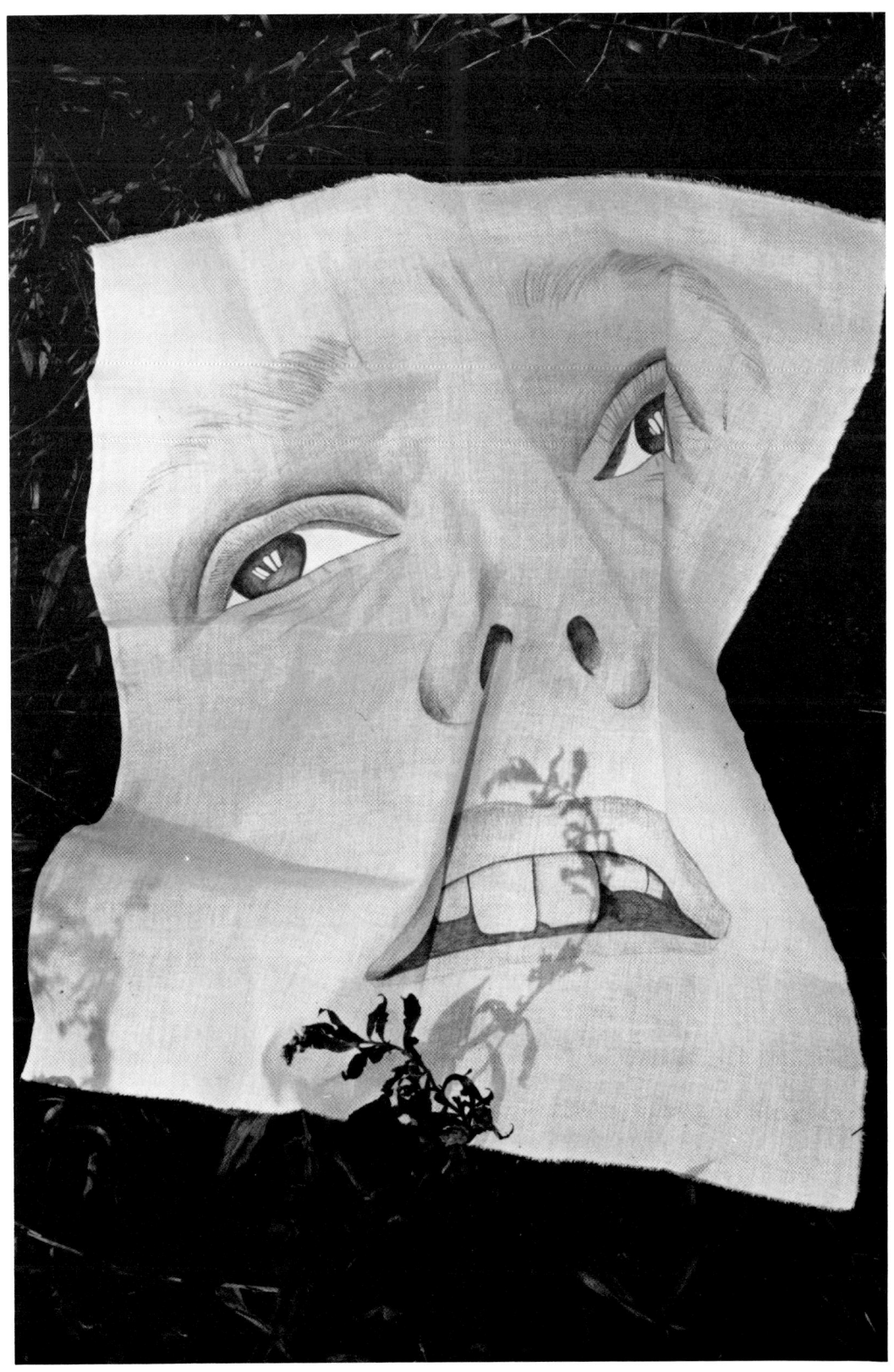

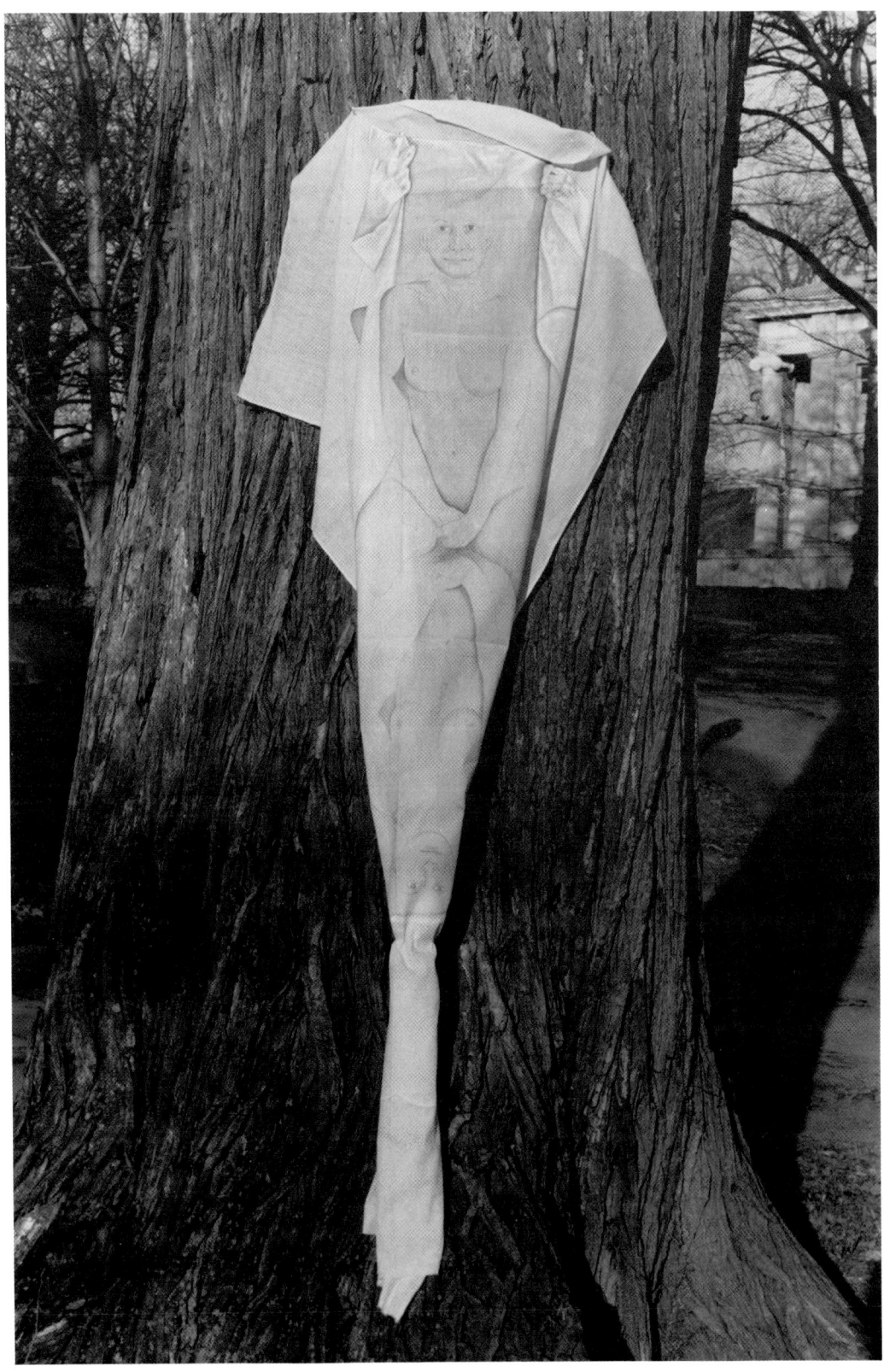

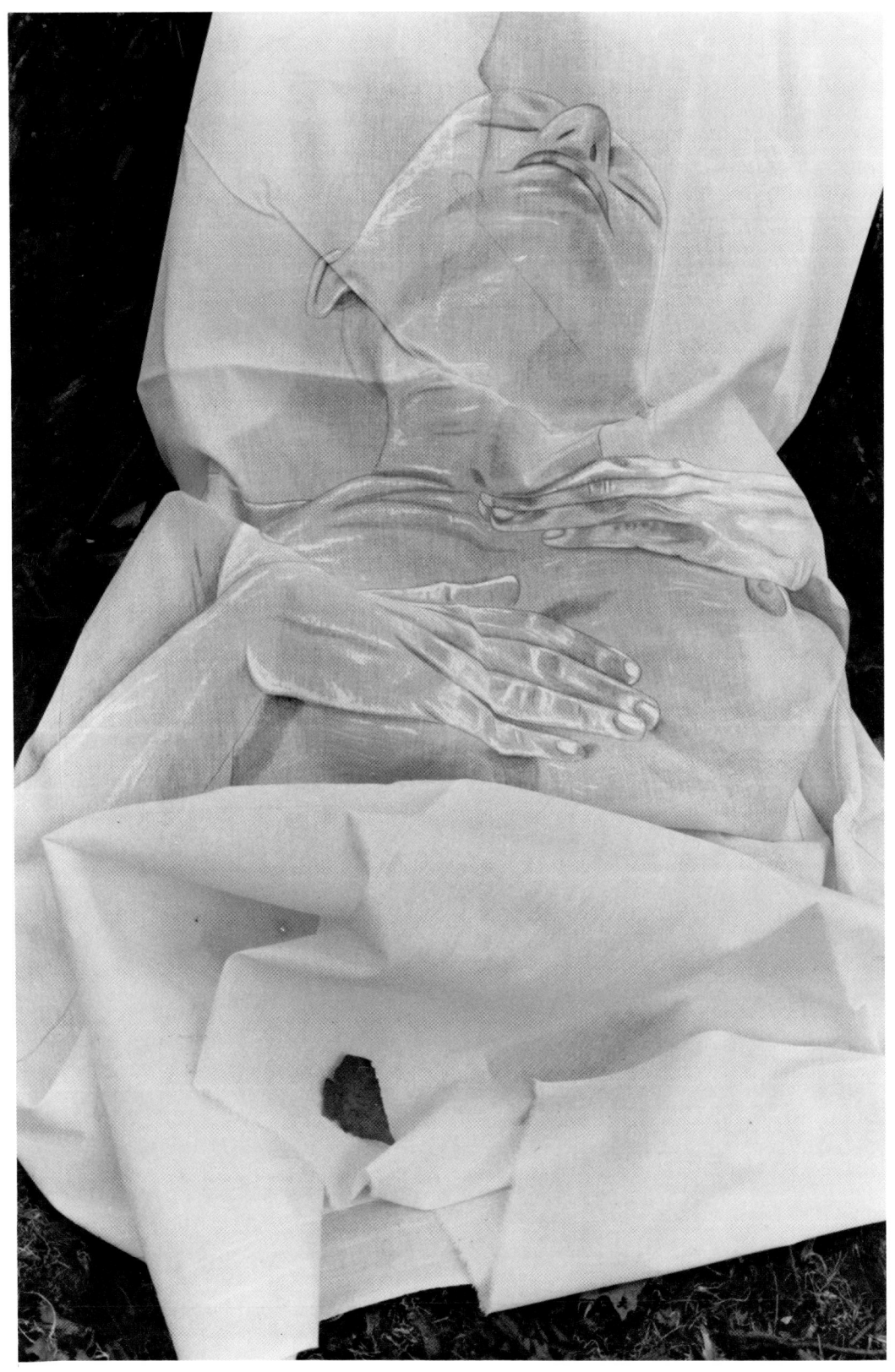

New York: Amsterdam Avenue at 111th Street

1986

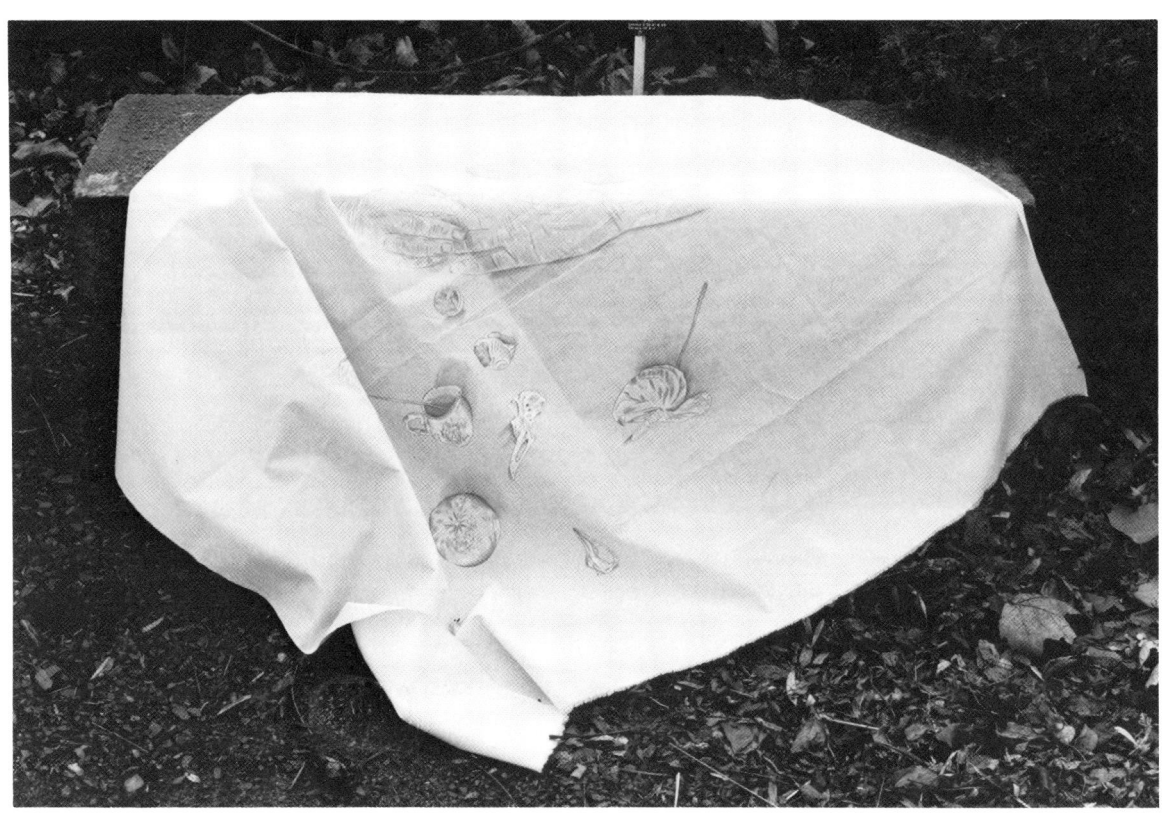

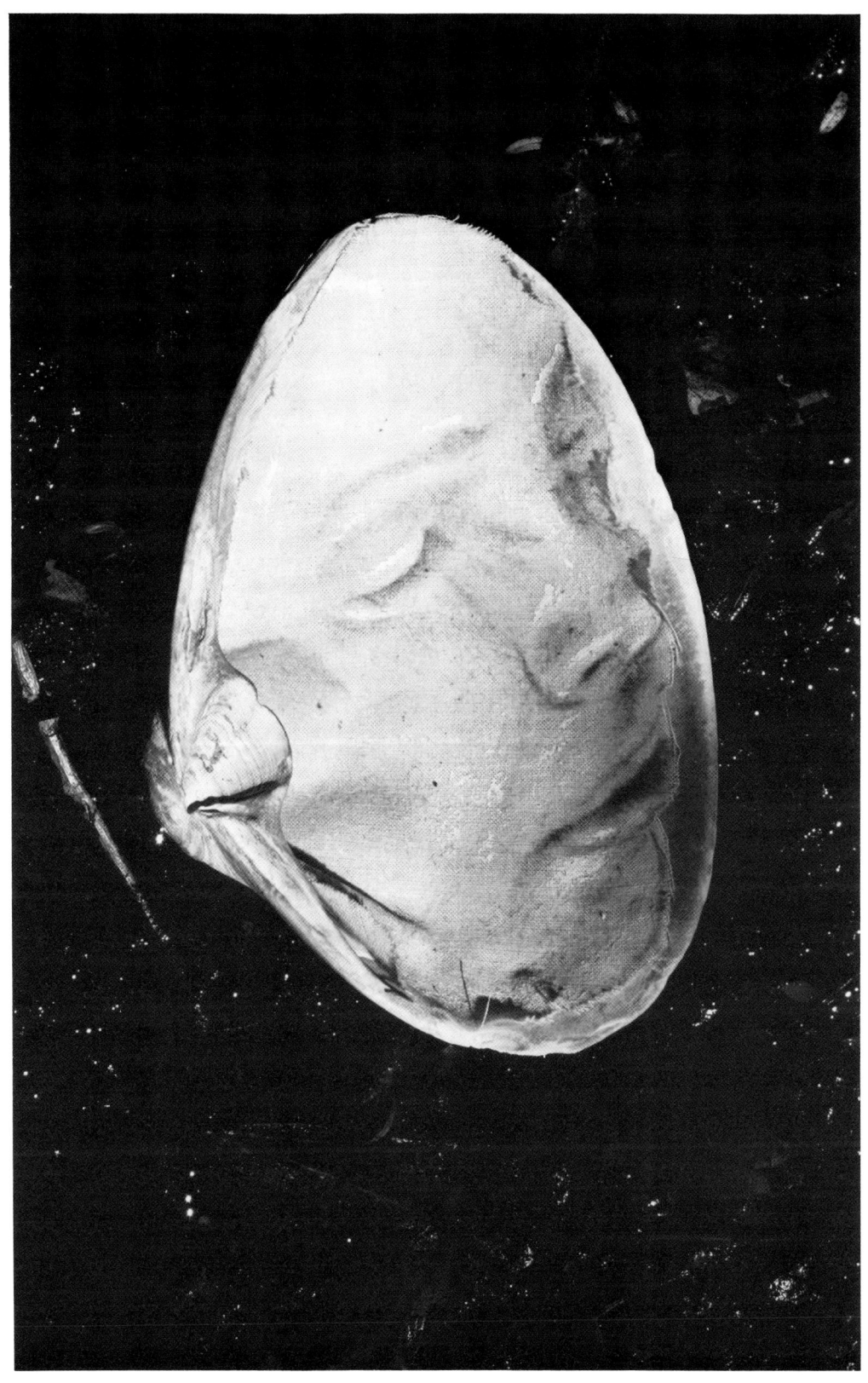

Winter Erotic

1985–1986

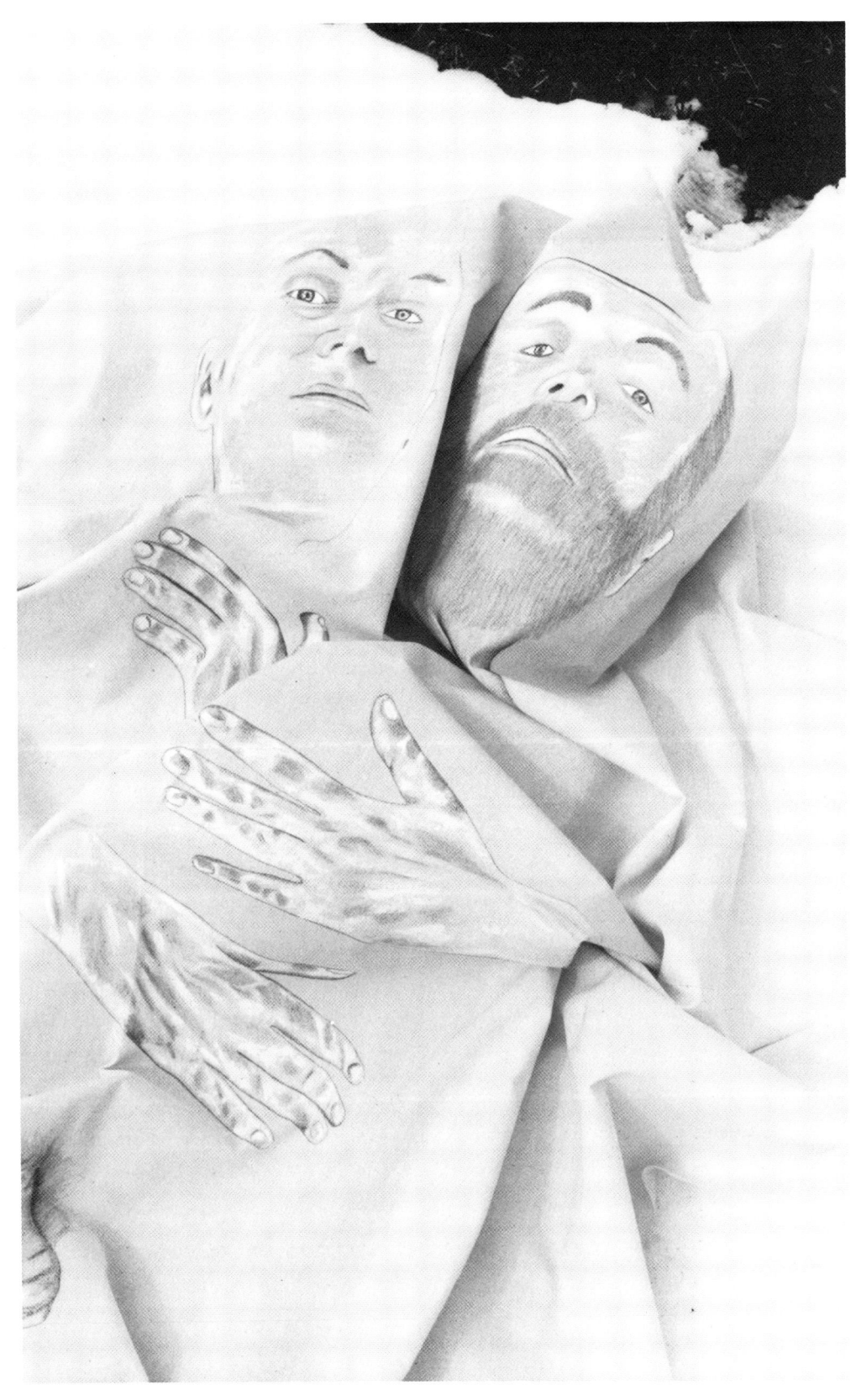

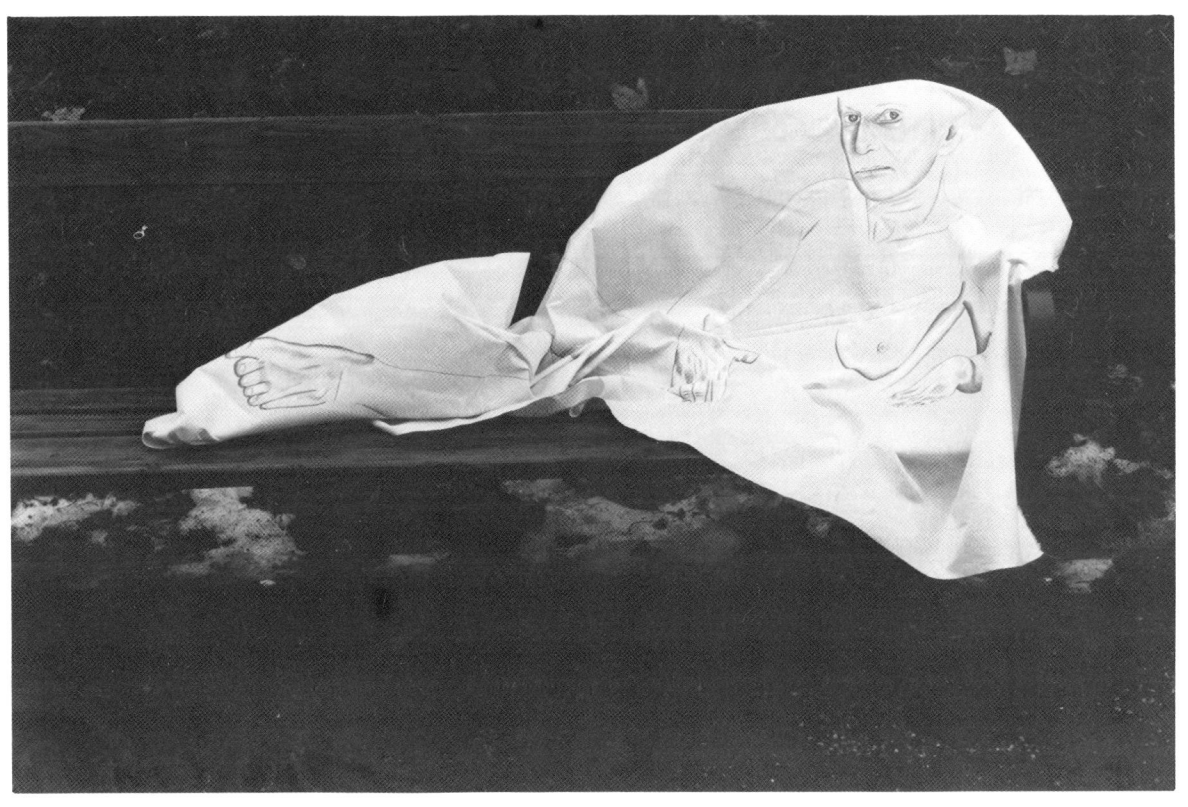

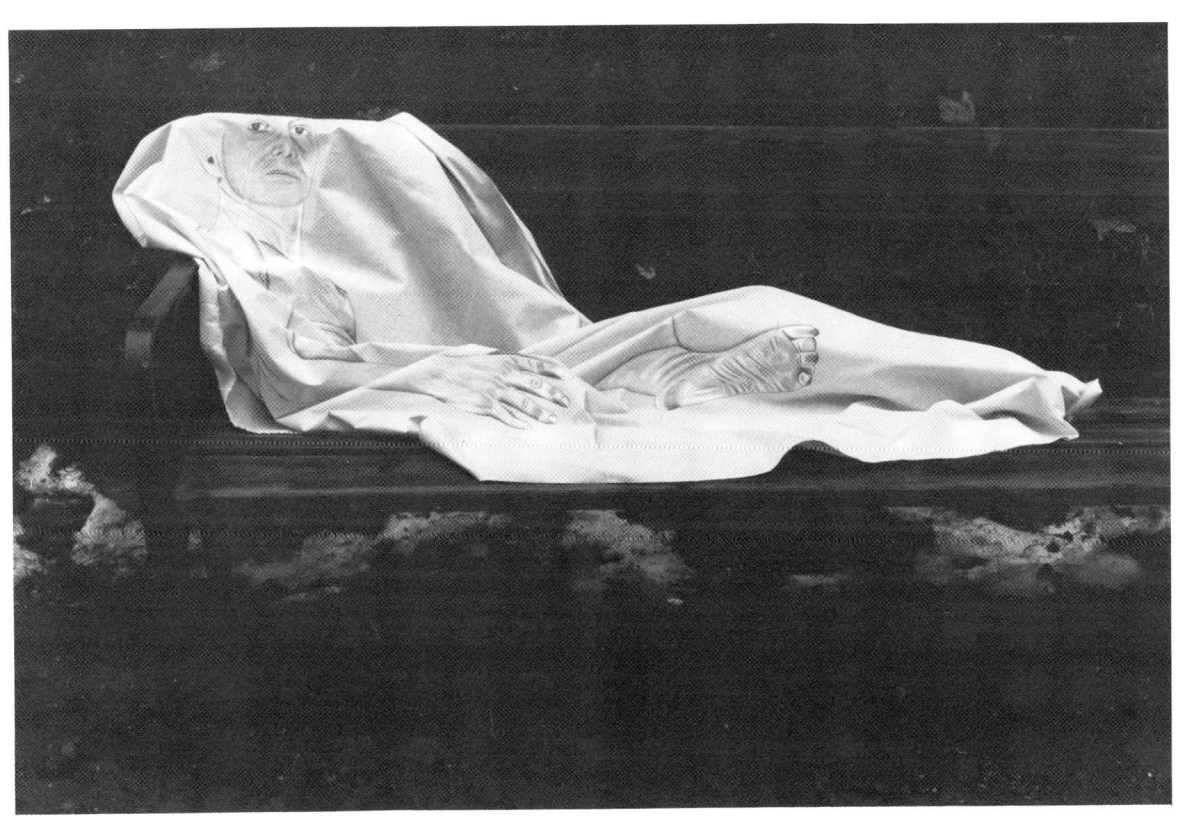

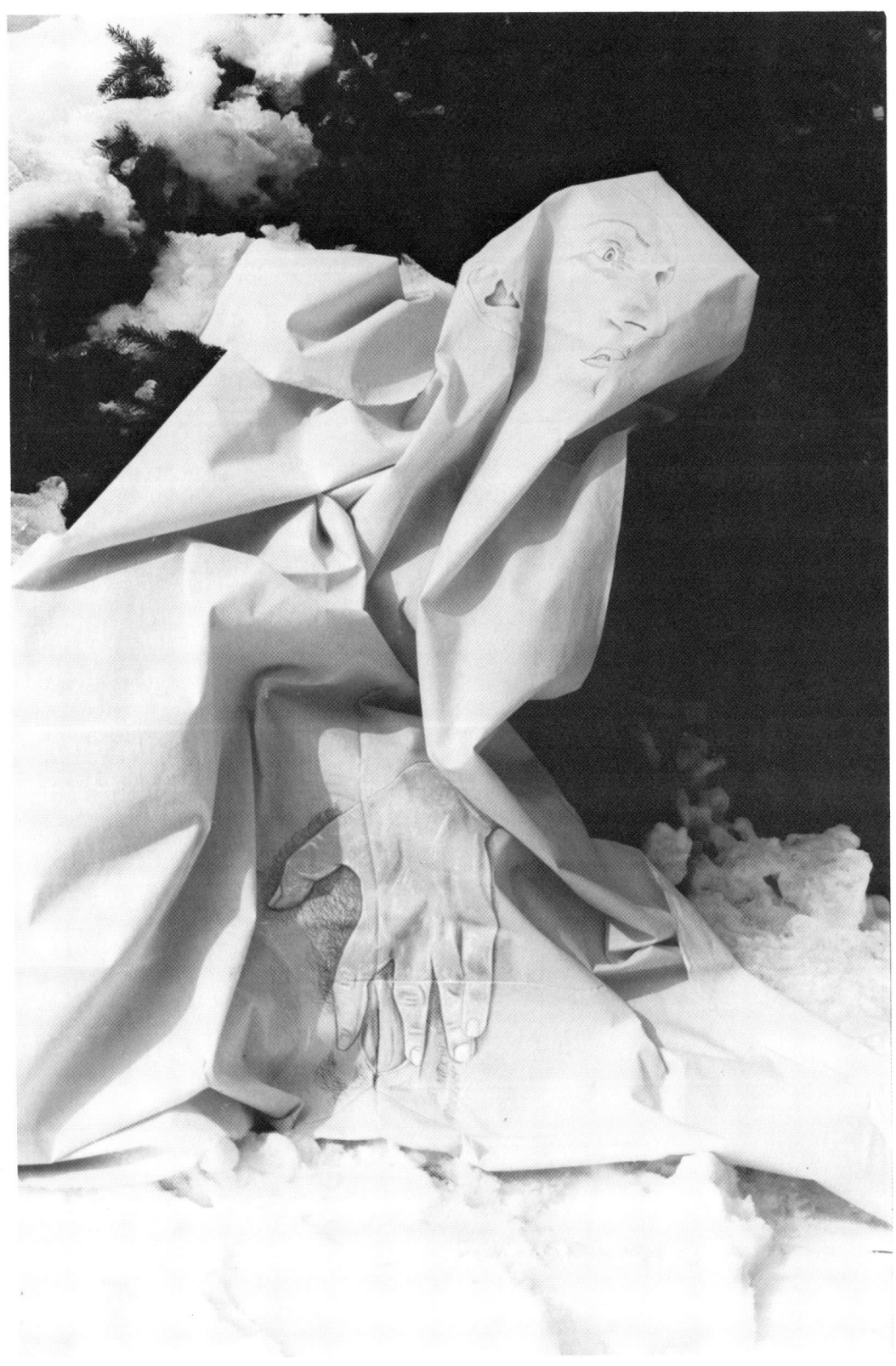

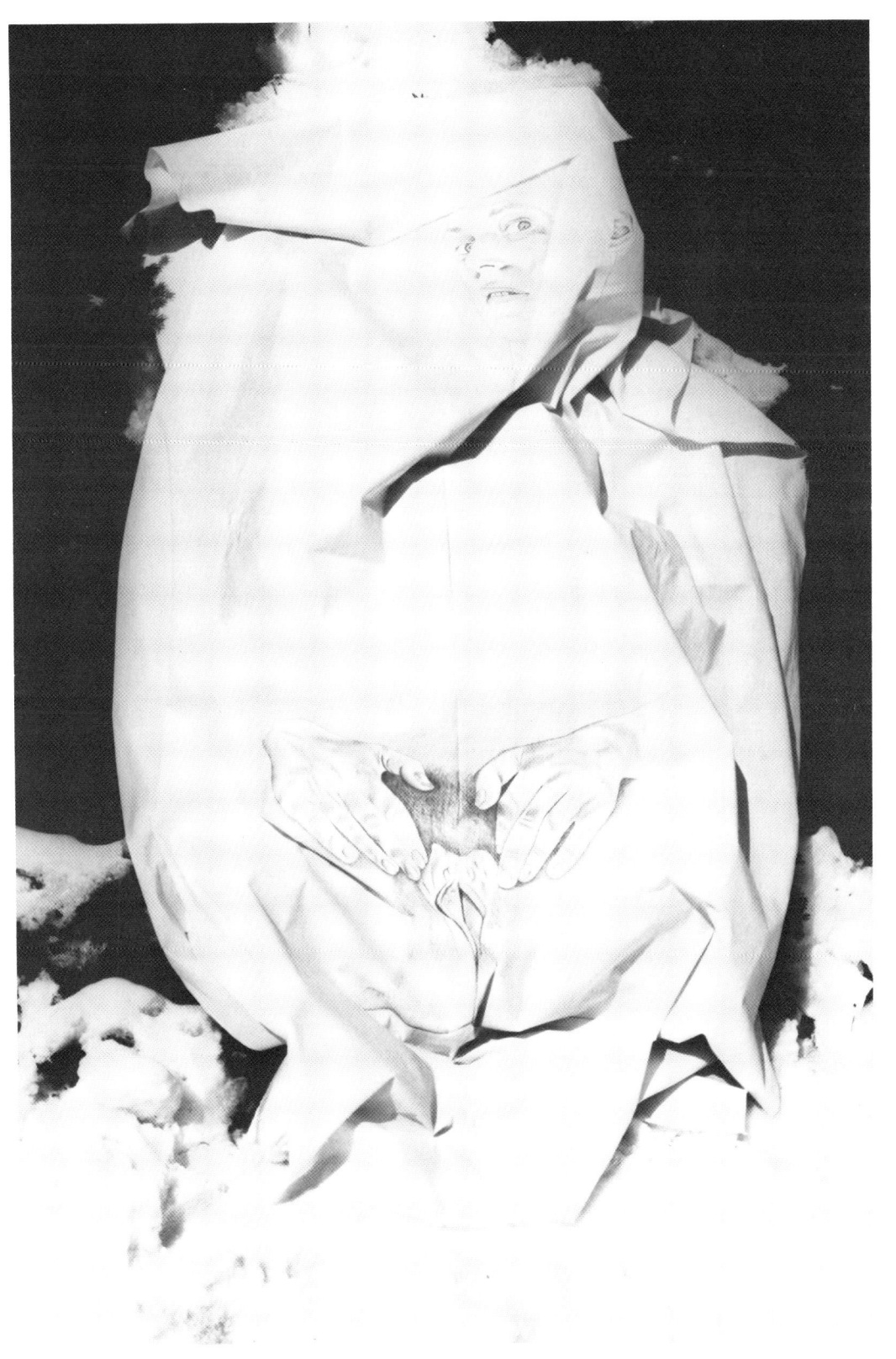

Catalogue of Works

All work is executed on unbleached cotton, unless stated otherwise, with a reddish felt-pen and white acrylic paint. All photographs were taken by Ewa Kuryluk, unless stated otherwise. When no collections are given, the work belongs to the artist.

page 37	*Cloth*, 1979, 43: 29"
page 38	*Cloth*, 1978, 43: 29¹/₂"
page 39	*Cloth*, 1978, 43: 29¹/₂"
page 40	Detail of *The Curtain*, 1979, 86¹/₂: 273"
page 41	Detail of the previous piece
page 42	*Brother with Butterfly*, 1978, 43: 29¹/₂"
page 43	Detail of the previous piece
page 45	*Tablecloth with Watch*, old linen, 1983, 11¹/₄: 15", collection Eva Hoffman, New York
page 46	*Tablecloth*, 1978, old linen, 8: 16", collection Martin Weinstein and Teresa Liszka, New York
page 47	*The Cup*, old linen, ca. 4: 4", private collection, USA
page 48	*Figure with Apples and String*, 1980, 78: 39¹/₂"
page 49	Detail of the previous piece
page 50	*Figure with Lilies*, 1983, 75: 39¹/₂"
page 51	*Figure with Book*, 1983, 78: 39¹/₂" (detail)
page 52	*Figure with Shells I*, 1983, 78: 39¹/₂"
page 53	*Figure with Shells II*, 1983, 78: 39¹/₂" (detail)
page 55	*The Couple I*, Standing Figure, 1981, 69: 15: 12", photo by Czesław Czapliński *The Couple II*, Standing Figure, 1981, 69: 15: 12", photo by Czesław Czapliński
page 56	*Figures with Masque*, 1981, 64: 47", one of two twin cloths
page 57	*Figures with Masque*, 1981, 64: 47", detail of the second twin cloth
page 58	*Theater of Love*, detail of the installation at Mobius, Boston, 1987
page 59	Detail of the previous piece
page 60	Detail of the previous piece
page 61	Cloth from *Theater of Love*, 1986, 69: 48"
page 62	Cloth from *Theater of Love*, 1987, 69: 48"
page 63	Cloth from *Theater of Love*, 1987, 69: 48"
page 65	*Female Figure with String*, 1982, 87: 32", from the installation *Las membranas de la memoria*, Centro de Arte y Comunicación, Buenos Aires, 1986
page 66	*Figure with Glass and String*, 1982, 85: 32"
page 67	Detail of the previous piece
page 68	*Squatting Woman*, 1979, 49: 25: 19", photo by Czesław Czapliński
page 69	*Squatting Woman*, 1979, 49: 25: 19", photo by Czesław Czapliński
page 71	*Body Book*, 1979, pieces of cotton, to be pressed and glued into a book on the walls of the studio
page 72	p. 3 and p. 7 of the *Body Book*
page 73	p. 11 and p. 12 of the *Body Book*, each page 11¹/₂: 8"
page 75	*Chairs*, 1982, from the installation *Las membranas de la memoria*, Centro de Arte y Comunicación, Buenos Aires, 1986
page 76-77	*Chairs*, 1982, three of twelve chairs, installation at the 12th International Sculpture Conference, San Francisco Bay Area, 1982. Cotton draped over white wooden chairs, each ca. 39: 16: 16"
page 78	Previous installation
page 79	Previous installation
page 80	Previous installation
page 81	Previous installation
page 82	Previous installation
page 83	Previous installation
page 84	*Shroud*, 1981, ca. 61: 20: 17"

page 85	*Two Shrouds*, 1981, each ca. 61: 20: 17"		part of the installation *Fall in Princeton* mounted at the banks of Carnegie Lake, Princeton, New Jersey, 1984	page 124	Another view of the previous piece
page 86	*Seated Man*, 1981, cloth draped over a wooden chair, 39: 16: 16", photo by Czesław Czapliński			page 126	*Amsterdam at 111th*, cloth draped over a chair, 1984, ca. 39: 16: 16", installation mounted in New York, 1986
		page 105	*Shroud*, 1981, ca. 61: 20: 17", from *Fall in Princeton*		
page 89	*Seated Man*, 1984, cloth draped over a wooden chair, ca. 39: 16: 16", photographed in the backyard of Nassau Court, Princeton, New Jersey, 1985	page 106	*Shroud*, 1981, ca. 61: 20: 17", from *Fall in Princeton*	page 127	*Shroud*, 1981, the same as shown on p. 85, detail of the previous installation
		page 107	*Woman in the Fall*, 1983, 58: 49", from *Fall in Princeton*	page 128	*Cloth and Stone*, Shroud, 1983, the same as shown on p. 98, from an installation mounted at Amsterdam and 111th, New York, 1986
		page 108-109	*Skin*, part of an installation mounted in the Princeton Woods, December 13, 1984, to coincide with the third anniversary of the imposition of martial law in Poland		
page 90	*Seated Man*, 1984, cloth draped over a wooden chair, ca. 39: 16: 16", photographed in the backyard of Nassau Court, Princeton, New Jersey, 1985			page 129	Another view of the previous piece
				page 130	*Shroud*, 1983, the same as shown on p. 99
page 91	Detail of the previous piece	page 110	Detail of the previous installation, each piece 70: 74"	page 131	*Shroud*, 1983, the same as shown on p. 98
page 92	*Man with Dog*, 1984, detail of a cloth draped over a wooden chair, ca. 39: 16: 16", photographed in the backyard of Nassau Court, Princeton, New Jersey, 1985	page 111	Detail of the previous installation	page 132	*Bottled*, 1982, 33: 33", collection Frances Brent, Chicago. Photographed at Amsterdam and 111th, New York, 1986
		page 112	Detail of the previous installation		
		page 113	Detail of the previous piece		
		page 114	*Faces*, 1981, each piece 25: 25", from *Fall in Princeton*, 1984	page 133	Detail of the previous piece
page 93	*Cloth with Man*, 1983, 70: 47", photographed in the backyard of Nassau Court, Princeton, New Jersey, 1985			page 134	*Tablecloth*, 1982, 60: 60", draped over a stone bench in the Biblical Garden, next to Saint John the Divine, New York, 1986
		page 115	*Face*, 1981, detail of previous installation		
page 94	*Views of Man*, 1984, 67: 47", photographed in the backyard of Nassau Court, Princeton, New Jersey, 1985	page 116	*Face*, 1981, detail of previous installation		
		page 117	*Face*, 1981, detail of previous installation	page 135	Detail of the previous piece
page 95	Detail of the previous piece			page 136	*Three Shells*, each ca. 4: 6½", cotton placed in shells, photographed in the Biblical Garden, New York, 1986
page 96	Detail of the previous piece	page 118	*Mirrored*, 1982, 87: 47", Campus of Princeton University, 1985		
page 97	Detail of the previous piece				
page 98	*Shroud*, 1983, ca. 38: 37: 17", photographed in the backyard of Nassau Court, Princeton, New Jersey, 1985	page 119	Lower detail of the previous piece		
				page 137	*Shell with Leila*, 1986, collection Eva Hoffman, New York, detail of the previous installation
		page 120	*Woman with Shroud*, 1981, 120: 47", Campus of Princeton University, 1985		
page 99	*Stranded*, Shroud, 1983, ca. 61: 20: 17", photographed in the backyard of Nassau Court, Princeton, New Jersey, 1985			page 138	*Shell with Wanda*, 1983, detail of the previous installation
		page 121	Upper detail of the previous piece		
		page 122	Lower detail of the previous piece	page 139	*Shell with Leszek*, 1982, in the artist's hand, photographed in the Biblical Garden, New York, 1986
page 101	*Man in the Fall*, 1984, 58: 49", from *Fall in Princeton*				
		page 123	*Spring in Princeton*, cloth, 1983, 51: 24", from an installation mounted at the banks of Carnegie Lake, Princeton, May, 1985		
page 102	*Woman in the Fall*, 1983, 53: 49", from *Fall in Princeton*				
page 103	Detail of the previous piece				
page 104	*Shroud*, 1981, ca. 61: 20: 17",			page 141	*Couple in the Melting Snow*, Double Shroud, 1985, 80:

	59", golf playground at Princeton University, from the installation *Winter in Princeton*, 1985		bench, Vienna, 1986	page 149	*Winter Erotic*, bedcloth, 1986, 69: 48", photographed in the snow, Vienna, 1986
		page 146	*Winter Erotic*, bedcloth, 1986, 69: 48", photographed in the snow, Austrian Alps, 1986		
page 142	Detail of the previous piece			page 150	*White*, three cloths, 1979, each 25: 25", from the winter installation, Vienna, 1986
page 143	Detail of the previous piece	page 147	*Winter Erotic*, bedcloth, 1986, 69: 48", photographed in the snow, Vienna, 1986		
page 144	*Odalisque*, 1986, 48: 69", draped over a wooden bench, Vienna, 1986				
		page 148	*Winter Erotic*, bedcloth, 1986, photographed in the snow, Vienna, 1986	page 151	Detail of the previous installation
page 145	*Odalisque*, 1986, 48: 69", draped over a wooden			page 152	Detail of the previous installation

Chronology

This chronology lists the major facts of Ewa Kuryluk's biography.

1946   Ewa Kuryluk was born in Cracow, Poland on 5 May.

1947   Her parents moved to Warsaw.

1959   Her family moved to Vienna where her father was appointed a diplomat. During the summer she began to paint and travel on her own, mainly by hitchhiking. She traveled with a group to Northern Italy and was particularly impressed with the Byzantine mosaics at Ravenna.

1960   She visited England.

1961   Kuryluk visited Paris and attended a summer course in French language and culture in St.-Mâlo.

1962   She attended summer courses at the University of Marseille in Nice. She hitchhiked along the Côte d'Azur and in Provence as far as the Spanish border.

1963   She traveled with a UNESCO youth program to Greece and hitchhiked from Athens to Delphi, Tiryns, and Mycenae. She became fascinated by ancient sculpture and particularly by tombstones—intimate depictions of people parting from each other—and the intricate beauty of marble folds.

1964   Kuryluk completed her Austrian *matura* and received a fellowship from the Italian Institute in Vienna to study Italian art and literature at the University of Urbino. She traveled in Umbria and Tuscany, descending as far as Rome in pursuit of twelfth and thirteenth-century paintings in whose iconography she was then interested.

She returned with her parents to Poland and began to study painting and graphics at the Academy of Fine Arts in Warsaw. Disagreeing with the way art was taught and defending her own style of painting—flat, colorful, hard-edged and autobiographical—she initially wanted to quit the academy but decided to remain. During this time she was in conflict with everyone and changed continuously from one master class to another.

1967   Rebelling against the rigidity of the system and the isolation of the students, she organized with two other colleagues an independent exhibition of their work on the staircase of the Academy. The show received publicity and was acclaimed by the distinguished art critic, Karolina Beylin, but it infuriated the professors. Further shows on the staircase were forbidden but she was granted a small space for "independent exhibitions" in the basement of the Academy. However, so many administrative burdens were imposed on her that she soon abandoned it. The idea was revived later by other colleagues who began showing art students' work in the foyer of PWSM (Academy of Music) and in the club of the Medical School.

She developed acute asthma and an allergy to oil paint and was granted, by medical prescription, the privilege to paint in acrylic, a new technique that was considered "Western" and suspect. Withdrawing from the Academy as much as possible, she worked mostly at home, began to write and publish her travelogues in the Warsaw magazine *Ty i Ja*, to translate into German for the magazine *Polen*, to illustrate children's books, and to work on her thesis in art history which became her first book, *The Viennese Apocalypse*.

1970   She received her diploma in painting and an M.A. in art history. She continued to study at the Jagiellonian University in Cracow. She participated in *O Poprawę (For Betterment)*, an artistic movement of the seventies.

1975   She visited the United States and wrote *Hyperrealism—New Realism*, a study comparing American and European art of the sixties and seventies.

1977–80   With four Warsaw artists of her generation, she formed the independent group, *Śmietanka (Cream)*.

Her large and colorful acrylic canvases, mostly self-portraits representing her in doubled and tripled form—the different selves in conversation with each other—were acquired by all major Polish museums, but external success coincided with an internal crisis. She abandoned painting and color and, searching for a new means of expression, began to draw, first on paper and then on diverse textiles. In a painful process of restriction, she finally began to work on wax-colored cotton with reddish felt-pens and acrylic white, finding with this her own medium: ephemeral, portable, and oscillating between drawing, painting, and sculpture. She taught as a Visiting Professor at the Film Academy in Łódź and the Catholic University in Lublin.

1981   She moved to New York and pursued in a new setting and language her former activities.

1981–7   Her cotton works were shown in the United States in one-woman and group shows. She established with other Polish émigrés the literary quarterly *Zeszyty Literackie* and served as the Corresponding Editor of *Formations*. In 1986 she taught on the faculty of the Justus-Liebig University, Giessen, West Germany. Her first book in English: *Salome and Judas in the Cave of Sex* was published by Northwestern University Press in April 1987.

Exhibitions

One-Woman

1987 *Theater of Love*, installation at Mobius, Boston, funded in part by a grant from the National Endowment for the Arts

1986 *Membranes of Memory*, Centro de Arte y Comunicación, Buenos Aires, Argentina

Imprints, Justus-Liebig University, Giessen, West Germany; Kunststation Kleinsassen, West Germany

1985 *Seven Black Chairs in the Snow*, outdoor installation on the campus of Princeton University

1984 *Villa dei Misteri*, installation, Art in General, New York

Fall in Princeton, outdoor installation on the banks of Carnegie Lake, Princeton, New Jersey

Skin, outdoor installation in the Princeton Woods, Princeton, New Jersey

1982 *Room of Memories*, installation, Helen Shlien Gallery, Boston

1980 *Fixed*, installation, Galeria Krytyków, Warsaw

1979 *Human Landscapes*, Art Gallery, Middlesbrough, England

Within These Four Walls, lining cloth installation, Ściana Wschodnia, Warsaw

1977 *Within the Confines of Human Landscape*, Galeria Nowa, Poznań

Paintings, National Museum, Wrocław

Paintings, Ściana Wschodnia, Warsaw

1976 *Paintings and Drawings*, Galeria Zapiecek, Warsaw

Paintings, Galerie Länderbank, Graz

1975 *Paintings and Drawings*, Galeria Pryzmat, Cracow

1974 *Tableaux*, Galerie Lambert, Paris

1973 *Paintings, Drawings, Prints*, Galerie Christian M. Nebehay, Vienna

Human Landscapes and Screens, Galeria Współczesna, Warsaw

1972 *Paintings, Prints*, Richard Bradley Atelier, Billingford, England

1970 *Paintings and Prints*, Woodstock Gallery, London

1969 *Paintings and Prints*, Galeria PWSM, Warsaw

Group Exhibitions

1986 *The Richard Demarco Gallery 20th Anniversary Exhibition for the 40th Edinburgh International Festival*, The New Richard Demarco Gallery, Edinburgh

1985-86 *The American Experience. Contemporary Immigrant Artists*, traveling exhibition curated by Cynthia Jaffee McCabe, Hirshhorn Museum, Washington, D.C.; Bass Museum of Art, Miami Beach; Balch Institute for Ethnic Studies, Philadelphia; Lakeview Museum, Peoria, Illinois

1985 *Textile Sculpture*, 12th International Biennial of Tapestry, Musée des Beaux Arts, Lausanne

Eastern Europeans in New York, El Bohio, New York

1984 *Art and Ego*, Pan Arts, New York

Art For Someone Else's Home, Fashion Moda, New York

1983 *Kleinsassen International 2*, West Germany

1982	12th International Sculpture Conference, San Francisco Bay Area		*Figurative Approach 2*, Fischer Fine Art, London		**Public Collections**

1982   12th International Sculpture Conference, San Francisco Bay Area

Arteder 82, Feria Internacional, Bilbao, Spain

1981   Bienal de Arte, Medellin, Colombia

International Drawing Biennale, Wrocław, Poland

Perspective, Illusion, Illusionism, National Museum, Warsaw

Garden of Knowledge, International Exhibition (curated by Ewa Kuryluk), Galeria MDM, Warsaw

Paintings and Drawings, BWA, Cracow

1980   International Art Fair, Basel, Switzerland

Labyrinth, curated by Wanda Siedlecka, Galeria MDM, Warsaw

Drawings and Commentaries, Contemporary Polish Drawing, Muzeum Okręgowe, Radom

1979   *Documents of Reality*, National Museum, Warsaw

Gallery's Artists, Ściana Wschodnia, Warsaw

Wojciech Skrodzki Presents: Drawing—the Ultimate Work of Art, Galeria Krytyków, Warsaw

1978   7th Festival of Fine Arts, Zachęta, Warsaw

Figurative Approach 3, Fischer Fine Art, London

Kinga Kawalerowicz Presents Symbolic Realism, Galeria Krytyków, Warsaw

Wojciech Skrodzki Presents Hommage to A. Matynia, Galeria Krytyków, Warsaw

1977   Traveling Exhibition of Contemporary Polish Art, Nevers and Reims, France

Figurative Approach 2, Fischer Fine Art, London

Śmietanka, Galeria MDM, Warsaw

To Be Continued, exhibition under the Poniatowski Bridge, Warsaw

1976   6th Festival of Fine Arts, Zachęta, Warsaw

I Love Hell, Galeria Stu w Teatrze Stu, Cracow

Jahr des politischen Gefangenen, organised by Amnesty International, Reinhardt-Seminar, Vienna

1975   *Generation XXX*, Galeria ZPAP, Warsaw

Kontraste, Rank Xerox Austria Drawing Competition, Österreichisches Museum für Angewandte Kunst, Vienna; Wolfgang-Gurlitt-Museum, Linz; Kunstverein Trakl-Haus, Salzburg; Opernhaus, Redutensaal, Graz

5th International Biennial Matmedia Exhibition, Dickinson State College, North Dakota

O Poprawę, Galeria ZPAP, Warsaw

Malerei, Zeichnung, Graphik, Skulptur, Galerie im Amerlinghaus, Vienna

Maitage, Ausstellungsgelände, Vienna

1974   *O Poprawę*, Galeria Teatru Studio, Warsaw

1972   4th International Graphics Biennale, Cracow

1969   *Graphics and Drawings by Students of the Warsaw Academy of Fine Arts*, Galeria Klubu Medyków, Warsaw

Public Collections

National Museum, Warsaw
National Museum, Cracow
National Museum, Wrocław
National Museum, Poznań
Museum of Modern Art, Łódź
Muzeum Okręgowe, Radom
Bibliothèque Nationale, Paris
Graphische Sammlung Albertina, Vienna
Kettle's Yard Museum, Cambridge, England
Bass Museum of Art, Miami Beach

Awards

1986   General Electric Award for an essay published in *Formations*

1985   Award of the Fund for Free Expression, New York

1984-85   Hodder Fellow, Princeton University

1983-85   Fellow at the Institute for the Humanities at New York University

1982   Fellow of the European Exchange Program, New York University

Room of Memories, installation at Helen Shlien Gallery in Boston, chosen the best show of 1982 by *The Boston Globe*

1964   Fellow of the Italian Institute in Vienna at the University of Urbino, Italy

Bibliography

Paweł Banaś, Preface to *Ewa Kuryluk, Catalogue*, National Museum, Wrocław, July 1977.

Stephen Bann, Introduction to *Ewa Kuryluk: 'Human Landscapes,'* Catalogue, Middlesbrough Art Gallery, April 28–May 19, 1979.

Oswell Blakeston, "Kuryluk, Woodstock Gallery," *Arts Review*, London, June 20, 1970.

Geneviève Bréerette, "Ewa Kuryluk: Mélanges," *Le Monde*, November 24-5, 1974.

Klaus Colberg, "Wenn die Fäden in den Raum greifen," *Mannheimer Morgen*, Mannheim, August 10, 1985.

Alicja Drwęska, "Letnie wystawy polskie," *Tydzień Polski*, London, October 1, 1977.

Rosa Faccaro, "Officiantes," *Il Clarin*, Buenos Aires, October 11, 1986, p. 35.

Dorota Folga-Januszewska, *Perspective, Illusion, Illusionism*, Catalogue, National Museum, Warsaw, April–May 1981.

Héctor Giuffré, "Ewa Kuryluk, un nuevo espacio escultórico," *Criterio*, Buenos Aires, June 14, 1984, p. 277.

Grace Glueck, "Ewa Kuryluk," *The New York Times*, April 13, 1984.

Jorge Glusberg, "Las membranas de la memoria de Ewa Kuryluk," *Catalogue*, Centro de Arte y Comunicación, Buenos Aires, October 1986.

Elżbieta Grabska, Preface to *Ewa Kuryluk: Textile Works*, Catalogue, BWA, Kielce, June 1981.

Halina Grubert, "W pracowniach Ewy Kuryluk i Krystiany Robb-Narbutt," *Express Wieczorny*, Warsaw, October 22, 1976.

Tomasz Gryglewicz, "Ekspresja i synteza," *Magazyn Kulturalny*, Cracow, no. 1, January 1976.

Maciej Gutowski, "Labirynt," *Kultura*, Warsaw, March 9, 1980.

Ewa Han, "Dzieło i odbiorca," *Odra*, Wrocław, No. 4, April 1978.

John Harvey, Preface to *Ewa Kuryluk: Paintings, Prints*, Catalogue, Richard Bradley Atelier, Billingford, May–June 1972.

Magdalena Hniedziewicz, "Zapis, Szkic, Dzieło," *Kultura*, Warsaw, April 22, 1979, p. 11.

Eva Hoffman, "From Poland, a New Breed of Emigre," *The New York Times Magazine*, May 20, 1984.

Margaret Hoggarth, "Ewa Kuryluk," *Arts Review*, London, no. 8, April 27, 1979, p. 215.

Irena Jakimowicz, Preface to *Documents of Reality*, Catalogue, National Museum, Warsaw, 1979.

–. "Rzecz o Rysunku," *Sztuka i Myśl*, The Second International Drawing Triennale, Catalogue, Wrocław, 1981.

W. E. Johnson, "A Pole Apart," *The Northern Echo*, Middlesbrough, May 18, 1979.

Jacek Juszczyk, "Krajobrazy wewnętrzne," *Gazeta Zachodnia*, Poznań, May 19, 1977.

Kinga Kawalerowicz, "Ewa Kuryluk," *Razem*, Warsaw, June 10, 1979.

–. "Rodowód pokolenia," *Kultura*, Warsaw, September 30, 1979.

–. "Malarstwo emocjonalne," *Kultura*, Warsaw, April 17, 1977, p. 11.

–. "Ewa Kuryluk," *Nowy Wyraz*, Warsaw, no. 10, 1979.

–. "Utrwalone przez Ewę Kuryluk," *Kultura*, Warsaw, November 16, 1980.

–. "Ogród Poznania," *Kultura*, Warsaw, July 26, 1981.

Barbara Koch-Münchmeyer, "Textile Skulptur," *Textilkunst*, Hannover, September 3, 1985.

Jan Kott, "Villa Dei Misteri," *Nowy Dziennik*, New York, April 5, 1984.

Milena Lamarova, "The 12th International Biennial of Tapestry," *American Craft*, October–November 1985.

Elżbieta Małkowska-Bator, "Niecodzienna codzienność," *Literatura*, Warsaw, April 26, 1979.

—. "Wystawa wspomnień," *Literatura*, Warsaw, October 16, 1980, p. 12.

Cynthia Jaffee McCabe. "Immigrants and Refugees: The Internationalization of American Art," *The American Experience. Contemporary Immigrant Artists*, Catalogue, Independent Curators Incorporated, New York, 1985.

Stefan Morawski, "O Niby-Realistach—Adiutantach Nowego Wieku," *Sztuka*, Warsaw, no. 5-6, 1979, pp. 1-5.

Sally Moren, "Painter leaves color for line drawing on draped cloth," *Princeton Weekly Bulletin*, April 15, 1985.

Terence Mullaly, "More Enterprise Outside London," *The Daily Telegraph*, London, May 5, 1979, p. 11.

Andrzej Osęka, "Dwie wystawy," *Tygodnik Demokratyczny*, Warsaw, June 24, 1973.

—. "Zärtlichkeit und Kälte," *Polen*, Warsaw, no. 7, 1975.

—. "Malarstwo nie ułądzone," *Tygodnik Demokratyczny*, Warsaw, April 4, 1976.

Joanna Paszkiewicz, "Kruchość Czterech Ścian. Rozmowa z Ewą Kuryluk," *Sztuka*, Warsaw, no. 5-6, 1979.

Mieczysław Porębski, Preface to *Tableaux de Ewa Kuryluk*, Catalogue, Galerie Lambert, Paris, November 1974.

—. "Ewa Kuryluk," *Pożegnanie z Krytyką*, (Cracow: Wydawnictwo Literackie, 1983), pp. 371-373.

Eileen Roche, "Metaphor For Caring," *Sojourner*, Cambridge, February 1982.

Zofia Romanowiczowa, "Silva Rerum Galerie Lambert," *Wiadomości*, London, July 15, 1979.

Jessica Scarborough, "Ewa Kuryluk," *Art New England*, February 1982.

—. "Ewa Kuryluk: Distillations in Fiber," *Fiberarts*, March-April 1985.

Joan Shepard, "Fabric of their lives on view," *Daily News*, New York, March 31, 1984.

Wanda Siedlecka, "Zamiast polemiki," *Kultura*, Warsaw, March 29, 1981, p. 12.

Wojciech Skrodzki, "The Reality of Shadow," *Projekt*, Warsaw, no. 4, 1980, pp. 42-46.

Juliet Standing, "Ewa Kuryluk. Richard Bradley Atelier," *Arts Review*, London, June 3, 1972.

Christine Temin, "Facing our common fate. Ewa Kuryluk, *A Room of Memories* at Helen Shlien Gallery," *The Boston Globe*, January 8, 1982, p. 22.

—. "Polish artist waits and hopes," *The Boston Globe*, January 8, 1982.

—. "Best," *The Boston Globe*, December 26, 1982.

Hugo Verlomme, "D'un ghetto l'autre," *Le Quotidien de Paris*, November 9, 1974.

Albino Dieguez Videla, "Ewa Kuryluk: la impresión del cuerpo," *La Prensa*, Buenos Aires, October 12, 1986.

Edmund White, "Strong Stuff," Introduction to *Villa Dei Misteri*, Catalogue, Art in General, New York, March 31-April 28, 1984; reprinted in *The Ontario Review*, no. 22, Spring 1985, and *Textile Sculpture*, Catalogue, Musée des Beaux Arts, Lausanne, June-September 1985.

Jana Wisniewski, "Textile Skulpturen in Lausanne," *Arbeiterzeitung*, Vienna, September 6, 1985.

Interviews and Writings by the Artist

"David Miller Talks With Ewa Kuryluk," *Mobius Newsletter*, vol. 4, no. 4, January-February 1987, pp. 6-7.

"Who's Afraid of the Little Red Mouse," *The Village Voice*, December 28, 1982.

"Dialogue with Ewa Kuryluk," *Sojourner*, Cambridge, December 4, 1982.

"On My Artistic Development Leading to Drawing on Fabrics," *Leonardo*, vol. 14, no. 4, Autumn 1981, pp. 265-770.

"Letters to W. Skrodzki," *Fixed*, Catalogue, Galeria Krytyków, Warsaw, September 1980.

"Drawing on Cloth," *Rysunki i Komentarze*, Catalogue, Muzeum Okręgowe, Radom, April-June 1980.

"Paintings," *TR*, London, no. 4, 1979, pp. 59-65.

Within These Four Walls, Catalogue, Ściana Wschodnia, Warsaw, February 1979.

"About my work," *Skira Annual*, no. 4, Geneva, 1978.

Ewa Kuryluk, Tomasz Ciecierski, Marek Konieczny i Jan Stanisław Wojciechowski, "O jarmarkach, domach towarowych i sztuce, dyskusja," *Literatura*, Warsaw, October 26, 1978.

Ewa Kuryluk, Wojciech Skrodzki, Kazimierz Wójcicki, "Mikrokosmos w lustrzanej karoserii," *Więź*, Warsaw, no. 7-8, 1978, pp. 121-128.

Within the Confines of Human Landscape, Catalogue, Galeria Nowa, Poznań, May 1977.

"The Genesis of a Painting. Instead of Introduction and Programmatic Formulations," Catalogue, Galeria Pryzmat, Cracow, 1975.

"Romantic Cycle: Human Landscapes—Realistic Cycle: Screens," Catalogue, Galeria Współczesna, Warsaw, May 1973.

Books by Ewa Kuryluk

Salome and Judas in the Cave of Sex (Evanston: Northwestern University Press, 1987)

Pani Anima (Cracow: Wydawnictwo Literackie, 1984)

Podróż do Granic Sztuki (Cracow: Wydawnictwo Literackie, 1982)

Kontur (Cracow: Wydawnictwo Literackie, 1979)

Hiperrealizm—Nowy Realizm (Warsaw: WAIF, 1979)

Salome albo o Rozkoszy (Cracow: Wydawnictwo Literackie, 1976)

Wiedeńska Apokalipsa (Cracow: Wydawnictwo Literackie, 1974)